CHARACTERS

A one-year exploration of the Bible
through the lives of its people.

VOLUME TWO

The Deliverers

LifeWay Press® • Nashville, Tennessee

EDITORIAL TEAM

Brandon Hiltibidal
Director, Discipleship and Groups Ministry

Brian Daniel
Manager, Short-Term Discipleship

Joel Polk
Editorial Team Leader

Dwayne McCrary
Content Developer

David Briscoe
Content Developer

G.B. Howell Jr.
Content Developer

Rob Tims
Content Editor

Laura Magness
Content Editor

Gena Rogers
Production Editor

Darin Clark
Art Director

Denise Wells
Designer

Lauren Rives
Designer

From the creators of Explore the Bible, Explore the Bible: Characters is a seven-volume resource that examines the lives of biblical characters within the historical, cultural, and biblical context of Scripture. Each six-session volume includes videos to help your group understand the way each character fits into the storyline of the Bible.

ISBN 978-1-4300-7036-8 • Item 005823504
Dewey decimal classification: 220.92
Subject headings: BIBLE. O.T.--BIOGRAPHY / LEADERSHIP--BIBLICAL TEACHING

We believe that the Bible has God for its author; salvation for its end; and truth, without any mixture of error, for its matter and that all Scripture is totally true and trustworthy. To review LifeWay's doctrinal guideline, please visit lifeway.com/doctrinalguideline.

Scripture quotations are taken from the Christian Standard Bible®, Copyright © 2017 by Holman Bible Publishers. Used by permission. Christian Standard Bible® and CSB® are federally registered trademarks of Holman Bible Publishers.

To order additional copies of this resource, write to LifeWay Resources Customer Service; One LifeWay Plaza; Nashville, TN 37234; fax 615-251-5933; call toll free 800-458-2772; or order online at LifeWay.com; email orderentry@lifeway.com.

Printed in the United States of America

Groups Ministry Publishing • LifeWay Resources
One LifeWay Plaza • Nashville, TN 37234

CONTENTS

About Explore the Bible 4

How to Use This Study 5

SESSION 1: *Moses: The Reluctant Deliverer* 8

SESSION 2: *Joshua: The Conquering Deliverer* 22

SESSION 3: *Deborah: The Unlikely Deliverer* 36

SESSION 4: *Samson: The Flawed Deliverer* 50

SESSION 5: *Ruth: The Redeemed Deliverer* 64

SESSION 6: *Esther: The Brave Deliverer* 78

Tips for Leading a Small Group 92

How to Use the Leader Guide 94

Leader Guide 95

ABOUT EXPLORE THE BIBLE

The Whole Truth, Book by Book

Explore the Bible is an ongoing family of Bible study resources that guides the whole church through the only source of the truth on which we can rely: God's Word. Each session frames Scripture with biblical and historical context vital to understanding its original intent, and unpacks the transforming truth of God's Word in a manner that is practical, age-appropriate, and repeatable over a lifetime.

Find out more at goExploreTheBible.com.

HOW TO USE THIS STUDY

This Bible study includes six sessions of content for group and personal study. Regardless of what day of the week your group meets, each session begins with group study. Each group session utilizes the following elements to facilitate simple yet meaningful interaction among group members and with God's Word.

INTRODUCTION
This page includes introductory content and questions to get the conversation started each time your group meets.

GROUP DISCUSSION
Each session has a corresponding teaching video to introduce the story. These videos have been created specifically to teach the group more about the biblical figure being studied. After watching the video, continue the group discussion by reading the Scripture passages and discussing the questions that follow. Finally, conclude each group session with a time of prayer, reflecting on what you discussed.

BIOGRAPHY AND FURTHER INSIGHT MOMENT
These sections provide more in-depth information regarding the biblical character being spotlighted each session and can be included in the group discussion or personal study times.

PERSONAL STUDY
Three personal studies are provided for each session to take individuals deeper into Scripture and to supplement the content introduced in the group study. With biblical teaching and introspective questions, these sections challenge individuals to grow in their understanding of God's Word and to respond in faith.

LEADER GUIDE
A tear out leader guide for each session is provided on pages 95-106. This section also includes sample answers or discussion prompts to help you jump start or steer the conversation.

VOLUME TWO

The Deliverers

MOSES

The Reluctant Deliverer

INTRODUCTION

What can cause a person to doubt his or her ability to accomplish a challenging task?

Some of our doubts come from a knowledge of our own abilities. We take a hard look at ourselves, and feel we aren't up to the challenge. Then again, some of our doubts come from the size of the task before us. We look at what we have been asked to do, and the obstacles seem insurmountable. We see both of these things in play in the life of Moses.

We are introduced to Moses in Exodus. He is mentioned many times in the New Testament, and is almost always shown in a positive light. Among God's people, Moses is rarely criticized. But when we meet him in the first chapters of Exodus, we get a picture of a reluctant and unsure person called to a giant task.

Moses initially let his feelings of inadequacy overwhelm him, but ultimately found his significance in the Lord. God worked powerfully through Moses to accomplish His will—despite Moses' doubt and fear. Therefore, Moses illustrates how God accomplishes His work through people like us—reluctant leaders, struggling sinners, feeble doubters, and weak workers. God loves and uses people, not because they are capable, but because He is capable.

How do our doubts feed our reluctance and hesitation to act?

What is the relationship between our fears and what we trust?

Watch the video teaching for Session 1 to discover "The World of Moses," then continue the group discussion.

FOCUS ATTENTION

Think of a time when you were completely out of your comfort zone. What fears did you have during those moments?

EXPLORE THE TEXT

As a group, read Exodus 3:4-16.

Characterize Moses' initial response when he observed the burning bush and realized something supernatural was happening. When have you realized a situation to be something that only God could do?

God identified Himself as the God of Moses' father, of Abraham, Isaac, and Jacob. What did this communicate to Moses? How should knowing God's name impact our willingness to follow Him?

What was the biggest mistake Moses made? How might we make the same mistake today?

As a group, read Exodus 4:13-16.

What causes people to hesitate to do what God asks them to do? How do these hesitations compare with Moses' excuses?

As a group, read Exodus 7:1-13.

Why was Moses' and Aaron's exact obedience so important? How does simple and complete obedience demonstrate faith?

As a group, read Exodus 14:21-31.

For the Israelites, what was the result of God working through Moses in such a dramatic fashion?

What larger impact did the Red Sea crossing and the defeat of Egypt have for Israel? For the surrounding peoples? For believers today?

APPLY THE TEXT

God calls and empowers people to serve Him and His purposes. God is holy, but demonstrates His grace by approaching and equipping unholy people. Believers can be assured that God provides the resources for them to be successful in their God-given responsibilities.

What role does God desire you to play in His redeeming of His people? What steps do you need to take to carry out the mission you have identified?

List resources God has given you to use to accomplish His will. How can you use each resource?

Reflect on Exodus 3:14. In what current situations do you need to be reminded that God is always true to His character?

Close your group time in prayer, reflecting on what you have discussed.

MOSES

KEY VERSE

No prophet has arisen again in Israel like Moses, whom the LORD knew face to face.

— Deuteronomy 34:10

BASIC FACTS

1. Son of Amram and Jochebed [JAHK uh bed] (descendants of Jacob through Jacob's son, Levi), who grew up to lead Hebrew slaves out of Egyptian slavery and gave them God's law at Mount Sinai.

2. Had two siblings: older brother Aaron; older sister Miriam.

3. Name *Moses* possibly of Egyptian origin, but also related to a Hebrew verb meaning "to draw out."

4. Name relates to two key events: (1) the infant Moses was drawn out of the Nile River in a papyrus basket by the Pharaoh's daughter; (2) Moses led the Hebrews' exodus (drawing out) from Egyptian slavery.

TIMELINE

1700 BC–1600 BC

- Body armor used in China 1700
- Minoans develop system of running water 1700
- Linear A script comes into use on Crete 1700
- Cookbook developed in Mesopotamia 1700
- Rhynd Papyrus (mathematical text) 1650

1600–1500 BC

- Volcano on Santorini erupts 1600
- War chariots used in Egypt 1600
- Miriam 1539–1408
- Aaron 1529–1407
- Moses 1526–1406

KNOWN FOR

1. While shepherding flocks in the wilderness around Mount Horeb (Sinai), Moses encountered the Lord God in a burning bush that was not consumed by the flames (Ex. 3–4). God told Moses to return to Egypt and lead the Israelites out of slavery to become a covenant nation and take possession of the promised land of Canaan.

2. After God sent plagues on Egypt, Moses miraculously led the Israelites through the Red Sea. They crossed on dry ground, but the pursuing Egyptian army drowned when the sea engulfed them (Ex. 14).

3. On Mount Sinai, Moses received God's covenant law in the form of the Ten Commandments on stone tablets (Ex. 20). These commandments laid out God's expectations on how the Israelites were to live as His people.

4. Throughout the Israelites' wandering in the wilderness, Moses served as the agent of God's liberation, provision, protection, and guidance (Ex. 16–17; Num. 11; 20–21).

5. Moses disobeyed God's specific instruction concerning one miraculous action— getting water from a rock by speaking to the rock rather than striking it with his staff—and was not allowed to lead the people into the promised land (Num. 20:6-13).

6. Moses climbed Mount Nebo at God's direction and saw the promised land. He died soon after at the age of 120, and God buried him in an unknown location in Moab (Deut. 34:1-7).

7. Moses contributed the first five books of Scripture (also known as the Torah, the Law, and the Pentateuch), as acknowledged by Jesus Christ (Mark 12:26; John 5:46).

1500–1400 BC

- Hittites develop iron technology 1500
- Glass bottles first used in Egypt 1500
- Joshua 1490–1380
- Israelites' exodus from Egypt 1446
- Ten Commandments given at Mount Sinai 1446
- Moses' death and burial on Mount Nebo 1406

1400–1300 BC

- Achaians establish early Greek civilization 1400
- Chinese develop multicrop agriculture 1400
- Division of land among Israelite tribes 1385
- Joshua's death and burial 1380
- Deborah 1360–1300

Trained in Pharaoh's House

By Gary P. Arbino

Moses was born during the New Kingdom period (1539–1075 BC), when Egypt was a powerful international empire and Pharaoh was its supreme ruler. When Moses was three months old, his mother hid him in a basket in the reeds of the Nile. Soon the "daughter of Pharaoh" discovered and adopted him (Ex. 2:3-10). "Daughter of Pharaoh" often refers to one of the pharaoh's secondary wives, rather than a biological offspring. The pharaoh's daughter adopted him and hired a nurse for him, in this case the child's Hebrew mother (vv. 5-9). Egyptian infants nursed for three years; afterwards the child returned to the royal house.

As a young boy, Moses would have spent most days playing. Swimming and riding lessons were common, as well as royal etiquette and table manners. Children also played with pets, especially dogs, cats, and monkeys. Egyptians spent leisure time listening to stories and wisdom tales, although most Egyptians had very little free time.

At the age of ten, boys began their formal education. Education in the New Kingdom was primarily for the elite class; most Egyptians were illiterate. Boys received the basics of a scribal education in reading and writing, which lasted four years. Moses would have also received instruction in archery, rowing, horsemanship, and perhaps basic military training.

When Moses was about fourteen, he would have received more specialized education for one of three basic career paths: military, government, and priesthood. At this point, Egyptians received schooling in writing the colloquial language of the New Kingdom as well as math, accounting, geometry, surveying, and basic engineering. Students entering the priesthood and the more intellectual careers received instruction in medicine, magic, dream interpretation, astronomy, and temple administration. For those who chose the military, advanced training included administration, geography, and foreign language. Although not stated in Scripture, we can assume that Moses received at least some instruction in most of these areas.

Gary P. Arbino, "Trained in Pharaoh's House," *Biblical Illustrator*, Winter 2003-04.

Nileometer on Elephantine Island. Nileometers were used to determine the height of the Nile River at flood stage.

By the time he was twenty, Moses would have completed his formal education. At this age, Egyptian culture would have dictated that Moses take an Egyptian wife. As an adult member of the extended royal family, he likely would have received either an assigned administrative task in the household or a minor office in local or provincial governance. When Moses was almost forty, this office may have been what took him out to see the Hebrews (see Ex. 2:11-12). What happened that day changed the course of his life.

Dated to about 1550–1295 BC, an 18th Dynasty painting from Thebes depicts a nobleman hunting in the marshes. The painting, which shows Nebamun, the "Scribe and Counter of Grain" fowling with throwsticks, is in the company of his wife and daughter aboard a light papyrus skiff. The daughter's haircut was a common style for Egyptian youth.

Illustrator Photo/ David Rogers/ British Museum/ London (7/13/10)

Illustrator Photo/ Bob Schatz (17/11/10)

Read Exodus 3:4-14.

God's people were enslaved for four centuries, but that would soon come to an end. God would use a surprising instrument to bring about their freedom. Moses was reared in privilege. During the time around his birth, the ruler of Egypt instituted a population-control decree. Pharaoh declared that the male children of the Israelites should be killed upon birth. Rather than obeying this wicked command, Moses' mother hid him, and the baby eventually was brought into the very house of the one who had issued the decree for his death.

Forty years later, Moses left the house of Pharaoh in disgrace, having killed an Egyptian for the way he was treating a Hebrew slave. During the last four decades, Moses had been a shepherd, but he had never seen anything like what he was about to experience in God calling him from a burning bush.

Moses found himself standing on holy ground. It must have shaken him to his core not only to see the burning bush, but to hear the voice of the Lord. In the midst of his fear, Moses also experienced God's grace and purpose, for no sinful man can survive a close encounter with God. How would Moses respond to such a revelation? For that matter, how should any of us respond to a holy God?

How does your understanding of God's holiness compare and contrast with that of Moses? How does growing in the depth of our understanding of God's holiness impact our walk with Him?

God is not required to reveal Himself to humanity, but chooses to do so out of love and for His purposes. Even so, God is holy and should be approached with reverence. God told Moses He would use him to orchestrate history-changing events that would become embedded in the minds of the Israelites as one of the most significant moments in their story as a people.

But Moses wasn't too sure. God commissioned him to do something that seemed impossible. Moses was sent by God to stand before Pharaoh and call for the Israelites' release. He was sent to lead a huge group of slaves out of bondage, and Moses knew he wasn't up to the task. Who was he to do this?

Moses is a prime example that God "is able to do above and beyond all that we ask or think" (Eph. 3:20). His purposes are accomplished by His power, not ours. God sent Moses as the deliverer to rescue His people from slavery and to lead them to dwell in the promised land. This would be possible only if God supplied the power. In other words, Moses was asking the wrong question. He should not have been asking, "Who am I?" but instead, "Who are You, God? Can You really accomplish this?"

Why is it important to take our eyes off ourselves and put them on God in matters of obedience? Why is this so difficult to do?

Moses did get to this question, and notice how God identified Himself—He is I AM. We might translate this another way: "I am the One who is." Simply put, God's nature is not dependent on anything other than Himself. God is beyond our exhaustive knowledge, and yet He graciously chooses to reveal Himself to us. While He is not completely comprehensible, by revealing His personal name, He shows that He is knowable. In this sense, the more you know about God, the more you do not know.

Hebrews 1:1-2 states, "Long ago God spoke to the fathers by the prophets at different times and in different ways. In these last days, he has spoken to us by his Son." Jesus is the clearest revelation of God to man. For this reason, the name I AM anticipates the "I am" sayings of Jesus in the Gospel of John, which show His deity (see, for example, John 8:58). Moreover, God's promise to be with Moses foreshadows Jesus' promise to be with the disciples as they went on mission with God (see Matt. 28:18-20).

Read Exodus 7:1-13.

After Moses agreed to be God's messenger, he followed God's directions. God laid out His strategy for bringing about His purposes in delivering His people. There are three reminders of God's promises from earlier conversations that fortified Moses and his brother Aaron in their calling and confidence. First, God reminded Moses that He had provided Aaron to function as a prophet before Pharaoh (see 4:14-16).

How would God's providing Aaron as a spokesperson bolster Moses' confidence?

Next, God again declared that He would harden Pharaoh's heart (see 4:21). Lastly, God proclaimed that He would bring Israel out of Egypt by His mighty hand (see 3:19-20). Neither Pharaoh nor his army would stop God from accomplishing His will. Pharaoh would know who God was when the plagues were unleashed against Egypt.

Without excuse, Moses and Aaron did exactly what they were told. We often shy away from God's work because of excuses or perceived weaknesses. But the example of Moses and Aaron in this passage reminds us that God's power is made most evident through our weaknesses. With confidence in our all-powerful God, we are called to live just as God has commanded us.

What attitudes toward God are demonstrated by Moses and Aaron's obedience? Compare and contrast these attitudes with that of Pharaoh.

Pharaoh refused to listen to Moses, so the cycle of miraculous plagues began (see 7:14–10:19). The water in the Nile River turned to blood. Then frogs, gnats, and flies overran the land. One plague caused the death of livestock. Another brought boils, while another brought deadly hail. Still another brought swarms of locusts; then a plague of darkness covered Egypt.

Moses announced each plague, and each arrived and departed exactly as he stated. As the plagues progressed, they became more devastating. Several times Pharaoh promised to let the Israelites go, but then refused to free the people when each plague ended. The plagues punished Egypt, showed the powerlessness of its gods, and demonstrated God's sovereignty.

Consider for a moment how far Moses had come. Early in his life, Moses lived in the palace and wanted for nothing. For the middle section of his life, he lived humbly in the desert as a shepherd. Then he was back in the house of Pharaoh, but this time being used as an instrument of God to perform His signs and wonders. It's quite a life trajectory, full of all kinds of twists and turns.

Why might God have waited until this moment in Moses' life to use him in this way? How do you think Moses' perspective was different at this point in his life?

Throughout his life, Moses underwent an emptying process to the point where he was wholly surrendered to the purposes of God. Such is the case with us. Our life experiences are not just happenstance, but rather part of God's work getting us *where* He wants us to be and *who* He wants us to be.

Read Exodus 14:13-28.

The people were free. Moses led them out of Egypt after the horrific tenth plague of the death of the first born. But just when all were ready to breath a sign of relief, Pharaoh once again changed his mind and sent his army to retrieve the former slaves. For Moses, here was yet another moment of crisis, with the Egyptian army bearing down on one side and the Red Sea on the other.

Moses' words to Israel, "Don't be afraid" (v. 13), were issued to bolster their confidence. The Israelites were to stand firm and see God work. The phrase "the LORD's salvation" (v. 13) describes the deliverance only God can provide. God would do what Israel could not do. For Moses, there was no hesitation and no argument as there had been at the burning bush years earlier. Moses had learned a thing or two about God, and he wanted the Israelites to know these things as well.

God told Moses to lift his staff and stretch it out over the sea. God would divide the sea so that the Israelites could go through the sea on dry ground. As Israel faced certain destruction, God delivered them by the power of His hand. What a humbling moment for Moses! He was the one holding the staff, but he had no claim on Israel's deliverance. He was merely the one God had chosen to work through.

How can you discern the difference between you trying to do something big for the Lord, and the Lord doing something big through you? Why is it important that you understand the difference?

The angel of God stood between the Israelites and the Egyptians. When the angel of the Lord appears in the Old Testament, he is depicted as acting and speaking for God Himself (see Gen. 22:11-18). The angel of the Lord appeared in a flame of fire (see Ex. 3:2), in the pillar of fire and cloud (see 13:21-22), on Mount Sinai (see 19:18), and in the tabernacle (see 40:38). In all instances, the angel of the Lord signified God's presence and protection.

How does the promise of God's presence give a person hope? How does the promise of God's presence impact a person's faith?

Was Moses surprised? Was he shocked at all when he stretched out his hand and saw God drive back the sea? We don't know for sure, but the Bible gives no indication that he was. Moses had seen God do the miraculous before; and here he was again, witnessing God's commitment to carry out His plans and purposes for His people. Because Moses believed God, he was obedient to God, and God did exactly what He said He would do.

What is the relationship between faith and obedience? Can a person have one without the other? Explain.

When the Egyptian chariots pursued the Israelites into the dry seabed, God caused them to swerve and stall. Even the Egyptians themselves realized that their confusion and difficulty was no coincidence; this was all happening because Israel's God was fighting for His people.

At the command of God, Moses extended his staff again, and the sea completely engulfed the Egyptian army in judgment. It is important to note God's justice here. The Egyptians had repeatedly rejected God and His warnings. Pharaoh repeatedly went back on his promise to release Israel. God gave several warnings, but kept His word.

In contrast to Pharaoh, we find Moses following God without hesitation. The once reluctant leader was now the one God used to deliver His people.

JOSHUA
The Conquering Deliverer

INTRODUCTION

What's the relationship between faith and obedience?

Suppose a friend told you she really believes in her doctor, but she never follows her doctor's counsel, takes any medication the doctor prescribes, or takes any of the tests she schedules. You might wonder whether such a person really believes in her doctor.

In a biblical sense, faith is more than an intellectual acknowledgment of facts. Faith is about trust. It includes a confidence to obey God. It means having a readiness to act on a conviction because we believe in the One who issued the command. If we truly believe in God, we will follow His commands. Anything less suggests doubt. At this intersection of faith and obedience we meet Joshua.

Joshua became the Hebrew leader after Moses died, a position that required courage and boldness. His first order of business was to lead God's people against the city of Jericho. God's battle plan was unusual, but as Joshua and the people followed it, they saw God bring an astounding victory. The wall of Jericho fell, the people took the city, and Joshua's legacy was cemented as one who not only claimed to believe God, but who put that belief into action.

When you are called upon to take a step of obedience, what obstacles frequently interfere?

What truths about God must we tell ourselves when the obstacles to obedience seem bigger than the rewards of obedience?

Watch the video teaching for Session 2 to discover "The World of Joshua," then continue the group discussion.

FOCUS ATTENTION

Many are at least mildly familiar with the story of Jericho. Was there anything in the video that surprised you about the world of Joshua?

EXPLORE THE TEXT

As a group, read Joshua 6:1-7.

List some instructions that are conspicuously absent for a military campaign such as the one planned. What does the absence of such instructions communicate about God?

If the ceremonial actions described in these verses didn't actually accomplish anything, why did the Lord have the Israelites perform them?

The outcome of the entire affair is announced to Joshua at the outset: God had already given Jericho, its king, and its warriors into Joshua's hand (v. 2). The extensive marching, blowing of trumpets, and shouting that the Israelites were to engage in reinforced for the Israelites that God gave the victory.

Do you think it was easy for Joshua and the Israelites to follow these instructions, given what they were facing? Why or why not?

As a group, read Joshua 6:12-21.

As the people prepared to take the city on the seventh day, Joshua gave them an explicit instruction regarding Rahab. Why was she singled out? How did her being protected by Joshua demonstrate God's grace?

What did Joshua direct the people to do with the items in the city? What were the consequences for disobedience? What was the significance of this action?

As a group, read Joshua 6:22-27.

Rahab's obedience to God led to salvation for her whole family. How might God use our obedience to have a great impact on others and bring more glory to Himself?

What has the Lord removed from your life that you have sought to rebuild? Is there something now that God is calling you to give up or not return to again? Why are we often tempted to return to areas where we know life is not found?

APPLY THE TEXT

God gives His people victory when they trust Him and obey His commands. A believer's obedience is a demonstration of trust in God. God's directives clearly specify the results of obedience and disobedience. God honors those who obey Him by providing them with a place of service in His kingdom.

Where do you feel the Lord calling you to do something you are unsure of? How does this passage encourage you toward obedience, even in the face of doubt?

Consider how Rahab's faith impacted her entire family. How might we extend the grace of God to others so that entire generations might be changed?

In what ways are you tempted to return to parts of your life before Christ, looking for life in dead places? What action will you take to submit this area to God and seek life in Him?

Close your group time in prayer, reflecting on what you have discussed.

JOSHUA

KEY VERSE

But if it doesn't please you to worship the LORD, choose for yourselves today: Which will you worship—the gods your fathers worshiped beyond the Euphrates River or the gods of the Amorites in whose land you are living? As for me and my family, we will worship the LORD.

— Joshua 24:15

BASIC FACTS

1. Son of Nun and grandson of Elishama [ih LISH uh muh], head of the tribe of Ephraim.

2. Born in Egypt during the time of Israelite slavery.

3. Originally named *Hoshea*, meaning "salvation." Moses later changed his name to *Joshua*, meaning "Yahweh is salvation" or "Yahweh saves."

4. Upon Moses' death, became Israel's God-appointed leader.

5. Died at the age of 110, having led the Israelites to enter, take possession of, and allot the promised land among the tribes.

TIMELINE

1600–1500 BC

- Volcano on Santorini erupts 1600
- War chariots used in Egypt 1600
- Miriam 1539–1408
- Aaron 1529–1407
- Moses 1526–1406

1500–1400 BC

- Hittites develop iron technology 1500
- Glass bottles first used in Egypt 1500
- Joshua 1490–1380
- Israelites' exodus from Egypt 1446
- Moses' death and burial on Mount Nebo 1406
- Israelites under Joshua destroy Jericho 1406

KNOWN FOR

1. Joshua led the Israelite forces in their first military battle after leaving Egypt; Israel defeated the Amalekites at Rephidim (Ex. 17:8-16).

2. He served Moses by taking care of the special tent outside the camp in which Moses worshiped and prayed (Ex. 33:11).

3. Joshua served as one of the twelve men Moses sent to scout the promised land. When ten of the scouts advised that the Israelites could not defeat the land's inhabitants, Joshua and Caleb pleaded with the people to trust in the Lord and go forward to take possession of the land. The people refused, and God decreed that of those twenty years of age and older, only Joshua and Caleb would enter the promised land (Num. 13–14).

4. On God's command, Moses commissioned Joshua to become Israel's next leader (Num. 27:12-23; Deut. 31:14-23).

5. Joshua led the Israelites to take possession of the promised land by trusting in God and obeying His instructions, beginning with the miraculous defeat and destruction of Jericho, a key fortified city. At the same time, he led the people of Israel to renew their covenant commitments such as male circumcision, observance of the Passover, and dealing with sin in the camp (Josh. 1–12).

6. In his older years, Joshua led the Israelites in assigning the twelve tribal territories, assigning six cities of refuge, giving a number of other cities to the Levites, and leading the people in covenant renewal at Shechem (Josh. 13–24).

1400–1300 BC

- Achaians establish early Greek civilization 1400
- Division of land among Israelite tribes 1385
- Joshua's death and burial 1380
- Deborah 1360–1300
- Deborah and Barak defeat Canaanites 1320

1300–1200 BC

- Rameses II rules in Egypt 1279–1213
- Shalmaneser I rules in Assyria 1264–1234
- Merneptah Stele mentions "Israel" 1208
- Gideon 1250–1175
- Gideon defeats Amorites 1200

Joshua: A Man on Mission

By C. Kenny Cooper

Joshua, the son of Nun, played a significant role in Israel's history. He was chosen to succeed Moses and lead God's people into the promised land. Several factors helped prepare Joshua for this great mission.

To begin, he served as Moses' servant. When the forces of Amalek threatened Israel at Rephidim, Moses called on Joshua to enlist an army and to fight (see Ex. 17:8-13), proving Joshua to be an obedient servant and a capable military leader.

The Bible next mentions Joshua going with Moses up Mount Sinai (see 24:13). While returning, Joshua heard the noise from the camp below and reported it to be the sound of battle (see 32:17). Joshua was the young servant who stayed with the tent of meeting when Moses went into the camp (see 33:7-11). His devotion to Moses led him to ask Moses to forbid Eldad and Medad from prophesying, a request Moses gently denied (see Num. 11:26-30).

The second preparation factor occurred when twelve spies surveyed the promised land. A man was selected from each tribe; Joshua represented the tribe of Ephraim (13:8). While ten spies told of strong armies and fortified cities, Joshua and Caleb pleaded with the people to possess the land (see 14:8). The report of the ten bred fear; the people wanted to return to Egypt. Because the people failed to move forward, the Lord pronounced a curse. All persons age twenty and older perished in the desert; their children would possess the land. Joshua and Caleb were exempted from this curse (see 14:30,38; 26:65). For forty years, the conquest was postponed. Conquering the land eventually fell to Joshua because of his firsthand knowledge of Canaan's geography.

Perhaps the most important factor that helped prepare Joshua was his being commissioned for the task. As Moses approached the end of his life, he asked the Lord to appoint a new leader. God chose Joshua (see 27:18-19).

C. Kenny Cooper, "Joshua: A Man on Mission," *Biblical Illustrator*, Winter 1990.

In his farewell address, Moses explained that God chose Joshua as their leader (see Deut. 1:38; 3:28). Moses gave Joshua a formal charge (see 31:7-8). Afterward, the Lord commissioned Joshua calling on him to be strong and courageous (see 31:23). After Moses' death, the people responded favorably to their new leader.

Joshua led the people into Canaan and ultimately divided the land by tribal allotments. After some time in the land, Joshua assembled the people and charged them to decide whom they would serve. His decision was firm, "As for me and my house, we will serve the Lord" (Josh. 24:15b, KJV). Joshua died at age 110, having fulfilled his work and mission.

Joshua and Moses went up on Mount Sinai for God to give instructions concerning the laws and worship the Israelites were to follow. Jebel Musa is one of several possible sites for Mount Sinai.

Illustrator Photo/ Murray Severance (74/Sinai)

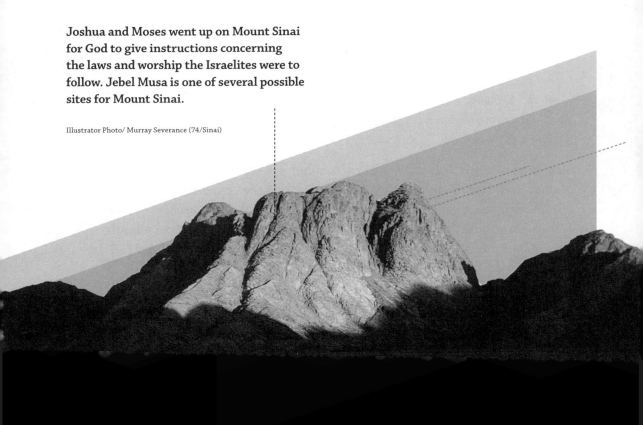

Read Joshua 1:1-9.

Before Jericho was conquered, Joshua was commissioned as the new leader of the Israelites. With the announcement that Moses was dead, God summoned His people to stop looking to the past and pointed them to the future. But even in looking to the future, God wanted Joshua and the people to know that victory was certain if they walked in faith. The Hebrews' possession of the promised land was as good as done because God promised it.

The commissioning of Joshua as Israel's new leader provided assurance of God's continuing presence. God's presence promised the Israelites complete victory over their enemies in possession of the promised land. As the Lord had been with Moses, He would be with Joshua.

How are God's presence and His promises connected? How does God's promise of presence change our perspective on a difficult circumstance?

Joshua knew a formidable task awaited him. Any person might have succumbed to fear and cowered when facing something like Jericho. But the Lord called Joshua to be strong and courageous.

The Hebrew verb translated "be strong" communicates the idea of physical strength. Joshua needed to be physically strong for the grueling events of the immediate future. The second verb, translated "be courageous," communicates the idea of confidence. Where would Joshua find the boldness to undertake this task in such an unexpected and unconventional manner? It could only come from the fact that the Lord had commissioned him and promised to be with him.

Both of these verbs, "strong" and "courageous," are commands. The Lord did not merely ask Joshua to be strong and courageous; the Lord commanded him to be strong and courageous.

God said Joshua would prosper by meditating on the Word of God. How does this apply to our lives today?

God instructed Joshua to keep and carry out His whole instruction. The Lord did not give Joshua the option of choosing to observe some of His laws while choosing to neglect others. Neither do we have the option of choosing to obey only the parts of the Bible we find to be easy, convenient, or agreeable to us. God expects us to be fully obedient to His entire written revelation. The Lord told Joshua that his success would depend on obedience to God's word. The success of believers in serving the Lord hinges on our obedience to the Word of the Lord as well.

Finally, the Lord told Joshua not to be afraid or discouraged because God promised to be with him in whatever he did. Our calling and commission may not be the same as Joshua's, but we can still trust God and His Word in all areas of our lives. When we accept the Lord's commission, trust in His Word, and count on His presence, we will find the courage to face whatever He calls us to do.

Why is it necessary for a leader to constantly be reminded of the truths found in God's Word? Should constantly being reminded of God's truths be any less important for those who are not the leaders? Explain.

Read Joshua 6:12-27.

Following God's specific instructions, Joshua led the priests in marching around the city of Jericho, escorting the ark of the Lord. The ark of the covenant was a chest about 4-feet long, 2 ½-feet wide, and 2 ½-feet deep. It held the stone tablets on which the Ten Commandments were inscribed. The ark was a visible reminder of God's presence with His people. The group returned to camp for the night (see 6:11) and repeated the march the next day.

The number "seven" characterized perfection to the Hebrews (notice seven priests, seven trumpets, seven days, seven circuits of the wall). The armed troops (in front) and rear guard (behind) protected the priests.

Joshua and the people patiently obeyed. It likely challenged their faith to adopt this particular strategy. However, obedience to God does not require a total understanding of His commands; it requires trust in God even when His entire purpose isn't seen.

What potential disasters await believers who refuse to wait for God's plan and timing? Does obedience always require patience? Explain.

Early on the seventh day, Joshua led the Hebrews in their final preparations for conquering Jericho. They marched around the city seven times in the same way as the previous days, carefully obeying the instructions of the Lord (see 6:4). After the seventh time, Joshua commanded the people to shout. Prior to this final pass around Jericho, the people had been told to be silent.

Joshua gave additional instruction that everything in the city would be set apart to the Lord for destruction. This commandment was not a new one; God had given it to Moses years before. In Deuteronomy 7:4, the Lord commanded Moses to destroy the people living in the promised land, knowing the inhabitants would lead the Israelites to worship other gods. (See also Deuteronomy 20:16-18.)

Joshua gave special instructions concerning Rahab. Rahab had shown kindness to the spies when she hid the men. The spies promised to protect her and her family when the Israelites destroyed Jericho (see 2:14-21). Interestingly, Rahab would appear in the genealogies of both David and Jesus (see Matt. 1:5,16). God not only spared Rahab's life, He gave her a prominent place in the genealogy of Christ.

Joshua gave a final warning regarding the material items inside Jericho. Wandering in the wilderness for forty years had left the Israelites a poor people. Joshua informed the people to keep themselves from the things set apart, or they would be set apart for destruction. Disobedience to this command would bring disaster on the Israelites. Achan disobeyed this command and kept some of Jericho's treasure. He paid for it with his own life and the lives of his family (see Josh. 7:1,16-26). God desires complete obedience from His people.

What do we steal from God that we should devote to Him (money, time, talent, etc.)? How does our withholding in these areas affect more people than just us?

The people shouted as the priests blew their trumpets. The trumpet blast heralded the moment of God's victory. We can only imagine the astonishment on the faces of the Hebrews as they watched the wall of Jericho collapse. Obeying the Lord's command, the Hebrews completely destroyed everything in the city. Unable to destroy the silver, gold, iron, and bronze, they put it in the treasury of the Lord's house.

How does obedience demonstrate what we really believe? Can we have genuine belief or faith without obedience?

Read Joshua 24:14-28.

With the promised land secured, Joshua once again acted with courage and boldness. Joshua summoned the Israelites to assemble at the central location of Shechem. He reminded them of their history, going back to the promise made by God to Abraham. Because the Lord had been faithful to His people, Joshua challenged them to be faithful to God. He challenged Israel to fear and worship the Lord.

The Hebrew word for "fear" can be interpreted as deep reverence and awe. The verb rendered as "worship" can be translated as "serve." Joshua challenged the Israelites to do more than simply respect, revere, and fear the Lord. He called on them to serve the Lord as well.

Joshua called on the Israelites to make a choice. They could choose to worship and serve other gods, or they could choose to worship and serve the Lord God. Joshua publicly proclaimed that his family would worship God, which became a model for the other Israelite households as well. Joshua's faithfulness set the standard.

No one can make another worship God; yet certain actions in households increase the likelihood that others will worship—or ignore—God (v. 15). Cite several examples of how your home can be one that serves the Lord.

The Israelites confirmed their commitment to the Lord. They remembered that their ancestors had once been slaves in the land of Egypt, and that the Lord delivered them through many great signs as demonstrations of His power. The Israelites also recalled that the Lord protected them in their journey to the promised land. He fed them with manna (see Ex. 16:11-18) and sustained them through many difficult circumstances. The people were grateful for God's provision and protection along their forty-year journey.

Their reflection on His provision and protection motivated the Israelites to remain faithful to Him. They would fully commit themselves to the One who delivered them from Egypt, provided for them in the wilderness, and gave them the promised land.

How does God's past provision serve as motivation to present and future faithfulness?

Joshua's reply probably shocked them. He knew the Israelites had a history of making commitments and not keeping them. He reminded the people that the Lord is a holy God, perfect in every way. God's people are to be holy because of God's holy nature (see Lev. 19:2).

Again, the people voiced their intentions to be faithful to the Lord. Joshua pointed out that everyone heard their public commitment; therefore, they served as witnesses against one another. The people accepted this responsibility.

Joshua instructed them to offer their hearts to the Lord. For the third and final time, the people committed themselves to the Lord. God had established a covenant with Abraham, Isaac, and Jacob (see Gen. 28:13). The Lord had further ratified that covenant at Mount Sinai with His people after He led them out of Egypt (see Ex. 24:1-8). Now, at Shechem, this covenant solidified the relationship between God and Israel.

Joshua instructed the people to turn their hearts to the Lord (v. 23). How is this mandate lived out through getting rid of other gods? Consider examples of gods in your life that get in the way of your sincerely following the Lord.

DEBORAH
The Unlikely Deliverer

INTRODUCTION

Some heroes pursue the role, but others stumble into the role or quietly accept it when it comes.

Accidental heroes become such unwillingly and perhaps even unknowingly. Unlikely heroes are those who don't initially appear to look or act much like heroes. They are not the kind of people from whom you would expect heroic deeds.

By and large, the Bible goes out of its way to highlight the stories of more accidental and unlikely heroes, rather than those who want to be known as such. Noah was a quiet and humble man, simply going about daily life as best he knew how in honor to God. Moses was a foreigner, living quietly as a nomadic shepherd, wanting nothing to do with God's rescue of His people. Rahab was a Gentile prostitute who believed God and chose to do a heroic thing in the advancement of His cause.

In the Book of Judges, we find at least one unlikely hero in Deborah. Deborah was a faithful and willing servant of God. She was a prophet, and she also is the only female judge in the Book of Judges. In a male-dominated leadership culture, Deborah emerges as an improbable heroine so that God can be known as the ultimate hero.

Are you more or less open to God using you in unusual or unexpected ways?

What are the advantages and disadvantages of being an unlikely hero as opposed to one more typically suited for the role?

Watch the video teaching for Session 3 to discover "The World of Deborah,"
then continue the group discussion.

FOCUS ATTENTION

Have you experienced the challenge of getting a group to buy into a vision? What possible reasons for hesitation exist for following a leader's strategy?

EXPLORE THE TEXT

As a group, read Judges 4:4-10.

The text calls Deborah a "prophetess" acting as a judge. How does this characterization differ from that of other judges in the book? Why is this distinction important.

Compare and contrast Deborah's role and Barak's role in the management of this crisis. Who looks more like a hero? Explain.

As a group, read Judges 4:11-16.

During the battle, who was credited with causing the victory? How did the victory come about?

As a group, read Judges 4:17-24.

Verse 24 states that after Sisera's death, "the power of the Israelites continued to increase against King Jabin of Canaan until they destroyed him." Why was this the case? Who in the story were the heroes who made this happen?

APPLY THE TEXT

Deborah's story is one of many in a long line of biblical narratives that highlight how God often chooses to work through accidental or unlikely heroes. With that in mind, consider the following questions.

What did Deborah do remarkably well as a heroine? What lessons can we draw from her story?

What might God be calling you to do that is outside your typical level of comfort or expertise? Pray how God might be working in you to be an unlikely hero.

Barak's hesitation affords an opportunity to evaluate our level of willingness to serve. On a scale of 1 to 10—with 1 being not willing and 10 being actively serving now—how willing are you to give yourself to what God is calling you to do? What evidence can you point to in support of your evaluation? What needs to change for you to increase your level of willingness?

Close your group time in prayer, reflecting on what you have discussed.

DEBORAH

KEY VERSE

"I will gladly go with you," she said, *"but you will receive no honor on the road you are about to take, because the* LORD *will sell Sisera to a woman."* So Deborah got up and went with Barak to Kedesh.

— Judges 4:9

BASIC FACTS

1. An Israelite woman, perhaps of the tribe of Ephraim, who lived during the time of the judges and provided much needed leadership during a time of spiritual compromise and oppression.

2. Hebrew name *Deborah* means "bee." Her parents are not identified in Scripture.

3. Wife of Lappidoth [LAP ih dahth], a man whose name means "flames" or "lights" and is named in Scripture only in Judges 4:4.

4. Served as a prophetess to and judge for at least some of the northern Israelite tribes—her seat of judgment located between Ramah and Bethel in the hill country of Ephraim.

TIMELINE

1500–1400 BC

- Hittites develop iron technology 1500
- Glass bottles first used in Egypt 1500
- Joshua 1490–1380
- Israelites' exodus from Egypt 1446
- Moses' death and burial on Mount Nebo 1406
- Israelites under Joshua destroy Jericho 1406

1400–1300 BC

- Achaians establish early Greek civilization 1400
- Division of land among Israelite tribes 1385
- Joshua's death and burial 1380
- Deborah 1360–1300
- Deborah and Barak defeat Canaanites 1320

KNOWN FOR

1. Deborah's service as a judge—at least in the beginning—appears to have been more of a judicial nature than a military deliverer of judges such as Gideon, Jephthah, or Samson (Judg. 4:5).

2. Given the patriarchal nature of ancient Israelite culture, Deborah's bold, faithful leadership is a measure of the poor state to which the men of Israel sunk during this time (Judg. 4:8-9).

3. After two decades of oppression of the Israelites by the powerful Canaanite king in Hazor, Deborah challenged an Israelite commander named Barak to gather troops and obey the Lord's command to fight against the Canaanite king's army. At Barak's request, Deborah agreed to accompany the Israelite forces into battle, but also warned Barak that a woman, not the commander, would receive the honor for defeating the Canaanites (Judg. 4:6-10).

4. Deborah prophesied that the Lord would give Barak and his forces victory over the Canaanite army (Judg. 4:14).

5. After the Israelite victory, Deborah and Barak led the people in a song of praise to God, affirming that Israel's leaders led, the people volunteered, and God gave the victory (Judg. 5).

1300–1200 BC

- Rameses II rules in Egypt 1279–1213
- Shalmaneser I rules in Assyria 1264–1234
- Merneptah Stele mentions "Israel" 1208
- Gideon 1250–1175
- Ammonites-Philistines 1170

1200–1100 BC

- "Sea Peoples" invade western Canaan 1200
- Jephthah 1200–1150
- Ruth 1175–1125
- Samson 1120–1060

Deborah and Barak

By Fred Wood

When the Israelites inhabited the promised land, many of their foes survived by finding refuge predominantly in rural areas. These enemies harassed the Israelites with raiding expeditions. God raised up military leaders to deliver the Israelites—leaders who usually became administrators in matters of equity and, thus, were called "judges."

Deborah came suddenly on the scene as both a judge and a prophet. We have no record of military events elevating her to the first position. Neither do we have a call experience that thrust her into the prophetic role. Among Israel's judges, Deborah alone is described as having the prophetic gift.

Concerning Deborah's "colleague in conflict," some have wondered, was Barak a mild-mannered man who required prodding or a brave man? Was he a coward or team player? Each reader must form his or her opinion from reading the text.

The Kishon River played a big role in Deborah and Barak's battle against Sisera (the Canaanite general) and his 900-chariot army. According to Judges 4, Deborah instructed Barak to lead 10,000 men to Mount Tabor. She promised that God would lead Sisera and his army to the Kishon. Barak agreed only if Deborah would accompany him. She consented, but warned that Barak would not be credited with the victory. Instead, God would deliver Sisera into the hands of a woman.

The battle's logistics seem simple. When Barak, with his ill-equipped army, saw the Canaanite forces advancing, he went to meet Sisera. God came to Barak's aid, unleashing the Kishon waters at the precise moment they were needed to bog down Sisera's chariots. Their sophisticated military equipment was completely inoperable.

Sisera fled, leaving his forces to face certain deaths. He ran to the tent of a loyal friend, Heber the Kenite. Heber was not there, but his wife, Jael, was. Using deception and trickery, Jael lured Sisera to her tent and delivered the fatal blow. Sisera died by the hands of a woman, just as Deborah had foretold. Two courageous females delivered Israel!

Fred Wood, "Deborah and Barak," *Biblical Illustrator*, Spring 2004.

Deborah's most important contribution was to show that God can and does use women in many areas of public and private life. She was a wife, which means she had household duties. Yet God used her abilities in other ways also. He did not speak to Israel during the Canaanite crisis through His Spirit or an angel, but through a woman. Barak also left a legacy. He worked with Deborah; they cooperatively won the victory.

Mount Tabor where Barak gathered an army against Sisera (Judg. 4–5).

Illustrator Photo/ Brent Bruce (60/9610)

Using a tent peg, Jael killed Sisera, a military leader for Jabin, the king of Hazor. This oak tent peg is approximately 2,000 years old.

Illustrator Photo/ David Rogers/ British Museum/ London (569/12A)

Read Judges 4:4-8.

After the brief description of the judge Shamgar and his success (see 3:31), the Israelites again rebelled against the Lord (see 4:1). The Lord allowed His people to be oppressed for 20 years by Jabin, king of Canaan. Jabin, his army equipped with 900 iron chariots, treated the Hebrews harshly (see 4:3). The Hebrews repented, and the Lord gave them the judge Deborah.

As a prophetess, Deborah was God's spokesperson to deliver His messages to the Israelites. Other prophetesses were Miriam (see Ex. 15:20), Huldah (see 2 Kings 22:14), Noadiah (see Neh. 6:14), Isaiah's wife (see Isa. 8:3), and Anna (see Luke 2:36). Nothing is known about Deborah's husband, Lappidoth. This is the only mention of him in Scripture.

In addition to prophesying, Deborah judged Israel. We typically think of a judge as a person who hears cases and renders decisions. The Israelite judges did this, but they also led and governed. Leaders in ancient times sometimes served as judges in rendering verdicts and settling disputes (as did Moses, for example; see Ex. 18:16). Israel's judges served as judicial, religious, and military leaders. Deborah served as God's spiritual spokesperson to Barak, who was Israel's military leader.

What can you glean about Deborah and her relationship with the Lord based on how she interacted with Barak?

Deborah summoned Barak and reminded him that the Lord had commanded him to deploy the troops on Mount Tabor. The word *summoned* implies authority that came from Deborah's calling as a prophetess for God. She delivered to Barak God's message, not her own ideas.

Deborah reminded Barak of the Lord's promise to lure Sisera, along with his army, to the Wadi Kishon. The word *wadi* describes a watercourse that is dry except in the rainy season. There, the Lord would hand Sisera over into Barak's hands (see vv. 13-14). Even though the Lord had promised to defeat Israel's enemy, Barak was still hesitant.

Why is willingness to serve essential in the life of a faithful believer?

Deborah clearly had the confidence Barak lacked, but even after her summons and reminders of the Lord's faithfulness, he was still in doubt. He would go fight only if Deborah agreed to go with him. What prompted Barak's hesitation? Was it cowardice? Was it failure to believe Deborah's (and the Lord's) assurance? Regardless of the reason, Barak recognized Deborah's status. We should read Barak's reply not only as a plea for Deborah's presence, but also as a plea for the presence of the Lord. Barak knew he needed God's leadership and presence that he saw in Deborah. He had to muster an army against Sisera, who had 900 chariots. Barak's army only had swords and spears to go against horses and chariots (see v. 13).

How does the presence of a person instill confidence? What makes confidence contagious?

Read Judges 4:9-16.

Deborah agreed to go with Barak. Her courage in going was essential to Barak's willingness to undertake the task. Deborah is an example—albeit an unlikely one—of how one person's courage in taking a stand for God gives courage to others in similar situations. Her faith was strong; there was no hesitancy on her part.

With the confidence he gained by Deborah's promised presence, Barak finally took action. He summoned the 10,000 men from the tribes of Zebulun and Naphtali. (Judges 5:14-15 indicates that additional soldiers came.)

Due to Barak's timid response to the Lord's command, Deborah told him that he would not be honored for the victory God would provide. Though Barak was the military commander, people would speak of Sisera's defeat at the hands of a woman. We might assume that Deborah was that woman, but we would be wrong. Judges 4:17-24 shows that a woman named Jael was responsible for killing Sisera.

God will not honor faithlessness. Nor will the Lord honor an unwillingness to serve Him. Faithfulness and willingness to serve are related in that our faithfulness moves us to service.

How is service an extension of a person's faith?

Scouts reported to Sisera that Barak had gone up to Mount Tabor. Located in the northeast section of the Jezreel Valley, Mount Tabor played a significant role in Israel's history. It served as a boundary point between the tribes of Naphtali, Issachar, and Zebulun (see Josh. 19:22). Although uncertain, Christian tradition identifies Mount Tabor as the place for the transfiguration of Jesus.

Sisera commanded his chariots and army to meet Deborah and Barak's forces. The chariot was an effective military machine greatly feared by opposing forces. For the Israelite army to attack iron chariots would be like sending infantry armed with outdated weapons against an army of tanks and supporting troops armed with the latest technology.

Deborah voiced no fear of Sisera's chariots. So sure of victory, Deborah insisted that the Lord had gone before Barak. The Lord not only goes with us, but also goes before us. Too often we decide what we will do and then ask God to bless our efforts. Instead, we should find out where God is going and go with Him. Genuine faith involves following God where He leads. Bolstered by Deborah's faith and presence, and to his credit, Barak advanced on Mount Tabor with 10,000 men.

How did Deborah's assurance of God's presence bolster Barak's willingness? How does the assurance of God's presence give a believer confidence?

The details of the battle reveal the victory as being won by the Lord. He determined the battle site. He threw Sisera and all his army into confusion. Why would Sisera abandon his chariot and flee on foot? Because the Lord sent rain to flood the wadi, rendering the chariots useless in deep mud (see Judg. 5:4,21). This incident reminds us of Pharaoh's chariots at the crossing of the Red Sea (see Ex. 14:25). Sisera's chariots of iron were powerful weapons under ideal conditions, but they were helpless when trapped in a sea of mud. With Sisera and his army in full retreat, Barak pursued them. At Harosheth, Barak defeated Sisera's whole army so thoroughly that not a single soldier survived.

Sisera alone escaped the battlefield. He made his way to the tent of Jael (the wife of Heber the Kenite, an ally of Sisera). Jael pretended to be a friend, invited Sisera into the tent, and gave him some milk to drink. When Sisera fell asleep, Jael used a hammer to drive a tent peg into his head (see 4:17-24).

How would you describe God's role in this battle? How do you differentiate between fighting for a cause and fighting alongside God?

Read Judges 5:1-11.

Words have often been used to paint pictures of praise to God. In Judges 5, the story of the Israelites' bold victory was told in the form of a praise song. This song is one of the oldest poems in the Old Testament. Scholars are not certain who wrote the song—perhaps Deborah. But verse 1 confirmed that both Deborah and Barak "sang" the song.

Deborah was the judge and Barak was the general, but God was the hero of this battle. This song deflected all the praise to God. Because the leaders were able to lead and the followers lent their full support, God was praised.

Despite their earthly power, it is God, not people, who will ultimately be praised. The song in Judges 5 called for kings and princes to listen. Deborah painted a word picture of God marching out as a Divine Warrior to help His people. She called for everyone to join in praising God.

What is the value of telling the story of God's mighty acts, particularly in song?

Their song is similar to that which Moses and Miriam sang after the destruction of the Egyptian Pharaoh's army at the Red Sea (see Ex. 15:1-18). Deborah is named first, as she appears to have been the leading singer (see 5:12). The lyrics of the song have some important things to say about godly leadership.

Godly and gifted leaders are something to praise God for! Moreover, following such leaders is to the people's credit and is evidence of God's favor. We can see a contrasting scenario in Hosea 13:10: "Where now is your king, that he may save you in all your cities, and the rulers you demanded, saying: 'Give me a king and leaders'?" People who put their faith in God are given good leaders; ironically, people who put their faith only in human leaders often find they are condemned to suffer under bad leadership. Deborah's song warns earthly rulers not to oppose the rule of God. When God is on the move, He cannot be resisted. The wisest course of action is to submit to Him.

How important is the role of leadership when it comes to God's plans being carried out?

Deborah's words are somewhat surprising with regard to the Lord coming from Seir. Seir is a mountain in Edom, the region south of the Dead Sea. Why would God be spoken of as coming from there? Probably the best answer is that it refers to the direction in which the ark of the covenant proceeded when the Israelites entered the promised land. Deborah's song looks back to the time when God made Mount Sinai shake, and when the Israelites marched through Edom, Moab, and into Canaan. God went before His people, giving them great victories.

How does remembering the past help us appreciate and understand the present?

Deborah returned to the theme of praising God for sending good leaders. She not only praised God, but also felt great kinship and affection for the leaders God called into action. She further exhorted the leaders themselves to praise God. Possessing donkeys often was seen as a badge of wealth, but it could also represent authority without pretense (see Zech. 9:9; John 12:14-15). The point is that those who have had success in leadership need to remember that their success is from the Lord. In the final analysis, the righteous acts of the Lord and the righteous deeds of His warriors in Israel are one and the same. It was the people who obediently followed and fought, and it was God who gave the victory. The people and their leaders together praised God. So should we today support godly leaders by praising the Lord for them.

SAMSON

The Flawed Deliverer

INTRODUCTION

What are the implications for not living up to our potential?

Every human life is full of potential. By responding to the nurturing care of their parents, many children will find their passion and begin to develop the skills needed to express themselves to their full potential.

Others, however, can also short-circuit their lives. Some with exceptional athletic ability fail to fine-tune their skills. Others with exceptional intelligence never really apply themselves. Still others forgo the discipline of rehearsal required of first-class musicians. People often compromise their potential by making unwise choices or allowing distractions to dominate their lives.

At the risk of oversimplification, that summarizes the judge Samson quite well. Samson frequently compromised his devotion to God by associating with the idolatrous Philistines. He found himself in constant turmoil and dispute with his oppressive neighbors. He relied on his physical prowess rather than humbling himself before the Lord. As a consequence, Samson was not as effective as he could have been. He failed to live up to his potential as a great servant of the Lord.

What role does spiritual compromise play in failing to reach one's full potential?

How does one compromise lead to another?

Watch the video teaching for Session 4 to discover "The World of Samson," then continue the group discussion.

GROUP DISCUSSION

FOCUS ATTENTION

What is the most memorable element of Samson's story to you?

EXPLORE THE TEXT

As a group, read Judges 16:4-6.

What clues do we have that trouble may be on the horizon for Samson?

What does Delilah making a deal with the Philistine leaders reveal about Samson's judgment and the people with whom he chose to associate?

As a group, read Judges 16:7-21.

How do you interpret Samson's continuing to offer Delilah the secret to his strength? Do you think he thought this to be a game, or was he simply naive?

How did Delilah's efforts sharpen over time? What does that teach us about the nature of the temptation to compromise?

How did sin blind Samson to the potential disaster awaiting him if he compromised? How does sin blind us?

What might cause a person to lose his or her spiritual sensitivity? How can we guard against losing our spiritual sensitivity?

As a group, read Judges 16:22-30.

How did Samson's physical blindness lead to spiritual insight?

How did God use Samson in spite of his flaws?

APPLY THE TEXT

God keeps both His promises and His warnings. Partnering with people who hold non-Christian values and beliefs often leads to spiritual compromise. How we treat temptation demonstrates our true love, either for God or for ourselves. God may remove His hand of protection from those who break His trust.

What criteria do you use for determining if you should or should not associate with a person, group, or institution?

What actions can we take to fend off temptation to compromise Christian beliefs? Which of these actions do you need to incorporate into your life?

Reflect on the truth that believers possess the permanent indwelling of the Holy Spirit to equip them to ward off spiritual compromise. How does that truth help you as you face temptation? What are you doing to put yourself in a position to more readily listen to the Holy Spirit?

Close your group time in prayer, reflecting on what you have discussed.

SAMSON

KEY VERSE

He called out to the LORD: "LORD God, please remember me. Strengthen me, God, just once more. With one act of vengeance, let me pay back the Philistines for my two eyes."

— Judges 16:28

BASIC FACTS

1. Son of Manoah [muh NOH uh] of the tribe of Dan.

2. Name *Samson* probably is related to the Hebrew word for "sun." The name's form suggests the meaning "little sun."

3. An angel of the Lord announced the child's birth to Manoah's wife, who was previously childless. She was instructed to place the child under a Nazirite vow from birth.

4. Judged Israel for a total of twenty years, particularly against the Philistines.

5. Died by pulling down a temple on himself and many Philistine worshipers.

TIMELINE

1300–1200 BC

- Rameses II rules in Egypt 1279–1213
- Shalmaneser I rules in Assyria 1264–1234
- Merneptah Stele mentions "Israel" 1208
- Gideon 1250–1175
- Ammonites-Philistines 1170

1200–1100 BC

- "Sea Peoples" invade western Canaan 1200
- Jephthah 1200–1150
- Gideon defeats Midianites-Amalekites 1200
- Ruth 1175–1125
- Samson 1120–1060

KNOWN FOR

1. Samson's mother was required to abide by the restrictions of the Nazirite vow during her pregnancy, so that Samson would not be disqualified from the vow before he was born. The vow further required that after the child's birth, Samson's hair was never to be cut. If the vow was honored, Samson would grow up to save Israel from the power of the Philistines.

2. Despite being an Israelite under a Nazirite vow, Samson had a fondness for Philistine women. He married a young Philistine woman from Timnah, which became an opportunity to confront and kill thirty men of his father-in-law's household (Judg. 14). When the father-in-law then gave Samson's wife in marriage to another man, Samson used a trick and the jawbone of a donkey to kill a thousand more Philistines (Judg. 15).

3. In Gaza, Samson slept with a prostitute and later fell in love with Delilah, a Philistine woman who lived in the Sorek Valley. Philistine leaders bribed Delilah to discover the secret of Samson's great strength. Samson tricked Delilah three times about the matter, but finally revealed that if his hair was cut he would lose his great strength. The Philistines cut Samson's hair while he was sleeping, gouged out his eyes, and then bound him with ropes to humiliate him as a slave (Judg. 16:1-20).

4. Samson's final act of valor occurred when he was taken to a Philistine temple for further humiliation. His strength (and his hair) had begun to return, so he prayed that the Lord might strengthen him for one more act of vengeance against the Philistines. Samson pulled down two supporting pillars, causing the temple to fall on and kill many pagan worshipers (Judg. 16:21-30).

1100–1050 BC

- Samuel 1105–1025
- Saul 1080–1010
- Death of Eli, priest at Shiloh 1070
- Twenty-first Dynasty in Egypt 1069–945
- Samson defeats enemies in death at Gaza 1060

1050–1000 BC

- Saul chosen as first king of Israel 1050
- David 1040–970
- David becomes king of Judah 1010
- David becomes king of all Israel 1003

Samson: Man of Triumph and Tragedy

By Robert D. Bergen

From beginning to end, Samson's life was one of superlatives. He was the youngest Nazirite in the Bible (see Judg. 13:5); in a culture where defying parents resulted in death, he brazenly rejected his parents' authority and prevailed (see 14:3); he also fought a lion and won (see 14:5-6); single-handedly he killed a thousand Philistine soldiers in one battle (see 15:15); he tore down a massive stone temple by himself in less than one day (see 16:30); and he is correctly described as the strongest man in the Bible. God worked mightily through this complex man; God's Spirit drove Samson "to save Israel from the power of the Philistines" (13:5), and when he acted he did so "by faith" (Heb. 11:32-33).

Samson's early years clearly show that he was a breaker, not a builder. He broke divine precepts by dishonoring—and disobeying—his parents (see Judg. 14:3-4; cf. Ex. 20:12), by touching an unclean animal's carcass (see Judg. 14:9; Lev. 11:24-25), and by marrying a pagan (see Judg. 14:8,10-18; Deut. 7:3). He broke his marriage apart (see Judg. 14:19b), broke Philistine bodies (see 14:19a; 15:15), the Philistine economy (see 15:5), and the Philistine city of Gaza's gates (see 16:3). Most famously, Samson broke his Nazirite vow when he had his hair cut through the wiles of the Philistine temptress Delilah (see 16:19); he also broke his vow by participating in a drinking party (see 14:10—the Hebrew word translated "feast" is derived from a word meaning "to drink"). Finally, he broke the Philistine temple honoring Dagon; and in doing so, broke his own body in death when the temple collapsed (see 16:23-30).

Although Samson's life was tragic in many ways, it was also one that showcased God's sovereignty. God brought Samson onto the stage of history during the dark days of the judges when the Israelites had spent decades under Philistine authority (see Judg. 13:1). In this era, the Israelites had accommodated themselves to a pagan, polytheistic people group in the promised land. The Israelites cooperated with the Philistine military (see 15:10-13) instead of fighting against them. And—as Samson himself demonstrated—they even intermarried with them (see 14:2).

Robert D. Bergen, "Samson: Man of Triumph and Tragedy," *Biblical Illustrator*, Spring 2019.

The Lord used Samson's strength and his unparalleled ability to create strife to sour the relationship that had developed between Israel and Philistia. The bond of cooperation between God's people and the uncircumcised Philistines—a bond that had been established over a forty-year period of time—was forever gone. The stage was now set for a period of sustained enmity between the two nations, a situation that would endure for more than 400 years, into the days of Judah's King Hezekiah (see 2 Kings 18:8). Samson's legacy would endure.

Iron shears from Egypt dating to the Greco-Roman Period.

Illustrator Photo/ David Rogers/ Field Museum/ Chicago (375/27A)

When the Spirit came upon Samson, he chased the Philistines to Ashkelon which was a central port city located on the Via Maris (Way of the Sea). There he slew 30 Philistines; shown, ruins of a Canaanite gate at Ashkelon.

Illustrator Photo/ Brent Bruce (86/B/0912)

Read Judges 16:1-15.

Samson slept with a prostitute in Gaza (Philistine territory). Desiring to kill him, the men of Gaza waited for the strong man to emerge. But Samson escaped Gaza at midnight. He later fell in love with Delilah, which opened the door for the Philistines to try a different strategy for subduing their enemy. They tried bribery, each promising Delilah 1,100 pieces of silver if she could discover and reveal to them the secret of Samson's strength.

Combined, the Philistine leaders offered Delilah 5,500 pieces of silver—an unheard of sum! For example, Jeremiah purchased a field for 17 pieces of silver (see Jer. 32:9), and 30 pieces of silver could purchase a slave (see Ex. 21:32). The amount of the bribe reveals the fear that the Philistines had of Samson.

Delilah made several attempts to discover Samson's secret. Samson offered Delilah an absurd reply in the first attempt, saying that if he were bound with bowstrings (cords made from animal intestines) that had not been dried, he would become as weak as any other man. The Philistines supplied Delilah with the strings and waited in an adjacent room to determine if Samson spoke truthfully. Delilah bound Samson with the strings. When alerted to the potential presence of Philistines, Samson snapped the strings.

On her second attempt, Samson told Delilah that if he were bound with new ropes, he would become as weak as any other man. Again, the Philistines supplied Delilah with new ropes and waited as Delilah bound Samson. But again Samson thwarted her efforts by easily snapping the new ropes (see v. 12).

What does Delilah's persistence communicate about Satan's desire to destroy our potential? How do we see this persistence today?

Verse 13 records Delilah's third attempt to discover the secret of Samson's strength. After Samson did not answer her direct question, Delilah acted in a cunning, calculating, and manipulative manner.

Delilah again accused Samson of mocking her and asked for the third time to reveal the source of his strength. As he had done previously, Samson offered an absurd reply. He told Delilah if she would integrate his hair with the fabric being woven on a spinning wheel, he would become weak. Samson courted disaster with this tease in that his hair was truly the key to his strength.

All three initial attempts got Delilah no closer to Samson's secret. In frustration, Delilah appealed to Samson's love for her. Consider the irony of this moment—she appealed to what she was pretending to be. Her actions reveal a love only for herself. Unfortunately for Samson, he failed to recognize that Delilah did not reciprocate his love. He allowed his feelings for Delilah to cloud his judgment to the extent that he made poor decisions and compromised his potential.

How might a person be manipulated to compromise his or her beliefs?
How does what you see in society today compare to the manipulation faced by Samson?

Read Judges 16:16-21.

Oblivious to the situation, Samson fell asleep on Delilah's lap. He would ultimately be destroyed in the very place where he felt the most secure, by the one in whom he placed his greatest trust.

Samson was willing to break his Nazirite vow to God and compromise his standing with the Lord for the love of a woman. The real tragedy in Samson's life occurred not when the Philistines subdued him, but when he compromised his potential by trusting a pagan woman rather than the Lord.

What types of situations might a person face today that would dull their spiritual sensitivity? How can a person strengthen or regain spiritual sensitivity?

Delilah's persistence ultimately overwhelmed Samson's resolve. Of the three requirements of the Nazirite commitment—abstaining from wine, not touching any dead thing, and not cutting one's hair (see Num. 6:1-8; Judg. 13:5)—Samson had kept only the last one. When describing himself as a Nazirite to God from birth, Samson used a generic word for God instead of the covenant name for the Lord, suggesting a lack of intimacy with God. He showed a spiritual blind spot by revealing his secret.

The Lord was the source of Samson's strength. When he lost the presence of the Lord, he lost his strength. But Samson didn't even realize it. It seems that his heart was so far from God that, apart from his lack of strength, he never would have noticed God's absence from his life.

In the Old Testament, the Holy Spirit empowered individuals for specific tasks. The Spirit took control of Samson, and he killed a lion with his bare hands (see 14:6; see also 15:14-15). When he failed to obey the Lord, the Spirit departed from him.

Since the coming of the Holy Spirit at Pentecost, Christians receive the indwelling Holy Spirit at the moment of salvation, and He remains in us permanently, providing eternal security (see John 10:27-29; 14:16-17). Nevertheless, by our disobedience we grieve the Holy Spirit and can hinder His work in and through us.

Samson was an imperfect instrument. He compromised his devotion to the Lord, yet God could still use him to deliver His people from their enemies. The lesson here is not that Samson is a model for Christians to follow; the lesson is the danger of spiritual compromise.

What weakness leads your heart astray and hurts your relationship with God? With others?

Who would be hurt if you compromised your spiritual integrity and commitment to the Lord? Does reflecting on these consequences help you remain faithful?

Read Judges 16:28-30 and Hebrews 11:32-34.

The Angel of the Lord consecrated Samson as "a Nazirite . . . from birth" (Judges 13:5). Two kinds of Nazirites are found in the Bible. Some took a Nazirite vow only for a specific period. Others were Nazirites based on a lifelong vow. In the New Testament, the apostle Paul is an example of the former (see Acts 18:18; 21:22-26). Samson and John the Baptist (see Luke 1:15-17) are examples of lifelong Nazirites. According to Numbers 6:1-21, Nazirites were prohibited from drinking wine (see vv. 3-4), cutting their hair (see v. 5), or touching any dead thing (see vv. 6-7).

The Nazirite vow is a key aspect for understanding Samson's life. He violated the prohibition against touching any dead thing when he scooped honey from the carcass of a lion he had killed (see Judg. 14:5-9). We are never told he drank wine, but we can assume he did as part of the wedding feast he hosted, since such occasions were characterized by wine consumption (see 14:10-12; John 2:1-11). The word for "feast" in Judges 14:10 comes from the Hebrew word meaning "to drink." Before his interaction with Delilah, Samson the Nazirite already had violated all but the prohibition against cutting his hair.

The Philistines captured Samson, gouged out his eyes, and imprisoned him in Gaza. He toiled in humiliation in their prison—but his hair began to grow. Meanwhile the Philistines celebrated their victory over Samson by worshiping their pagan god. They brought Samson to the celebration to gloat over his defeat.

When he was brought into a pagan temple to be mocked, Samson prayed to God for strength to take revenge on his enemies. Ironically, Samson asked God to "remember" him (16:28). In reality, Samson had forgotten God.

In what ways do believers in today's society forget God?

When have you forgotten God? How did God respond to you?

God responded to Samson's request. With his strength renewed for one final time, Samson brought down the pillars of the temple, killing himself and crowds of Philistines. Through his death, he accomplished more in fighting the enemies of the people of Israel than he did while he was alive.

The writer of Hebrews provided a list of examples of people who expressed faith in God. On a list that includes Gideon and David, we find Samson's name. When giving characteristics that set this group apart, the writer of Hebrews notes some who gained strength in their weakness and who administered justice. Samson certainly could be described in this way. We are reminded that the final word is not written about us until we breathe our last breath, giving us hope that this day may be the day we finally get it right.

How do these verses confirm that God can work through imperfect people? In what ways has God used your imperfections or your own humanness to make you stronger and more useful to His kingdom?

RUTH

The Redeemed Deliverer

INTRODUCTION

Sometimes life situations make us feel helpless and hopeless. Abandoned children often become victims in systems that fail to meet their needs. Widows spend long hours alone facing uncertain futures. Sudden illness interrupts an otherwise normal life.

These scenarios play out every day around the world. Even the most faithful followers of the Lord can be shaken, becoming disoriented in their spiritual walk and filled with despair. If left to themselves, they often make bad choices in an effort to cover the pain. These bad choices further complicate the problems.

The surprise twists of life can make us wonder if unexpected crises and catastrophes can derail God's plans and purposes for our lives. If we search, we find that God can restore us and bless us again. In the process, He can surprise us with whom He chooses to use to bring about His purposes. This is what happened to Ruth.

Ruth's story is one of tragic loss, but it's also a story of faithfulness. Ruth was faithful to her family and her God, and God was overwhelmingly faithful to her.

How can the promises of another person serve as a source of hope when facing a hopeless situation?

How does God's faithfulness in the hard times help you prepare for the good times?

Watch the video teaching for Session 5 to discover "The World of Ruth," then continue the group discussion.

FOCUS ATTENTION

Describe a situation in your life that seemed hopeless but turned around for good. How did you see God working through that experience?

EXPLORE THE TEXT

As a group, read Ruth 3:3-9.

What did Naomi instruct Ruth to do? Why was it important for Ruth to follow Naomi's instructions?

When Ruth followed Naomi's directions, what was Boaz's reaction? How did Ruth respond to him?

What connection did "Take me under your wing" have with Boaz's role as a "family redeemer"? How did the actions of Ruth demonstrate her character?

As a group, read Ruth 3:10-17.

How did Boaz respond to Ruth's request?

As a group, read Ruth 4:9-17.

What was the significance of listing Rachel, Leah, and Tamar in the blessing offered by the witnesses?

Ruth married Boaz, and God blessed them with a son, Obed. How did Ruth become a source of blessing for Naomi? How is she a source of blessing to people today?

APPLY THE TEXT

God can surprise us with those whom He chooses to use to bring about His purposes. Living with integrity leads to finding favor with God and others. Believers can face trials and challenges with confidence, knowing that God can use these for His honor and glory. God is always at work, making His redemptive plan known.

Discuss as a group the value of integrity in relation to our witness. What actions can the group take to foster integrity?

What opportunities is God placing in front of you that come out of trials and challenges you have faced? How can God use those trials and challenges for His honor? Ask Him to help you honor Him in your trials and challenges.

What role do you play in revealing God's redemptive plan to others?

Close your group time in prayer, reflecting on what you have discussed.

RUTH

KEY VERSE

But Ruth replied: "Don't plead with me to abandon you or to return and not follow you. For wherever you go, I will go, and wherever you live, I will live; your people will be my people, and your God will be my God."

— Ruth 1:16

BASIC FACTS

1. A young Moabite widow who accompanied her Israelite mother-in-law—also widowed—from Moab to Judah, where she married a relative of her mother-in-law.

2. Meaning of the name *Ruth* is uncertain; possibly means "refreshment" or "[female] companion."

3. Moabites were distant descendants of Abraham's nephew, Lot (Gen. 19:36-37).

4. By the time of the Israelites' entry into Canaan, Moabites worshiped idols and tried to have Balaam bring a curse on Israel (Num. 22:1-6).

5. As a result of her marriage to Boaz, Ruth became an ancestor of King David and Jesus Christ.

TIMELINE

1300–1200 BC

- Rameses II rules in Egypt 1279–1213
- Shalmaneser I rules in Assyria 1264–1234
- Merneptah Stele mentions "Israel" 1208
- Gideon 1250–1175
- Ammonites-Philistines 1170

1200–1100 BC

- "Sea Peoples" invade western Canaan 1200
- Jephthah 1200–1150
- Gideon defeats Midianites-Amalekites 1200
- Ruth 1175–1125
- Samson 1120–1060

KNOWN FOR

1. Ruth and her sister, Orpah, married the two sons of an Israelite couple, Elimelech and Naomi, who had fled from Judah to Moab because of a famine. Tragically, Elimelech and his two sons died, leaving the three women as widows (Ruth 1:1-5).

2. When Naomi decided to return to her homeland, Ruth insisted on accompanying her, making a lifelong commitment to stay with and care for Naomi as well as to worship the God of Israel (Ruth 1:16-17).

3. Once in Judah, Ruth met Boaz, a relative of Naomi's late husband, when she was gleaning for leftover grain in his barley field. Boaz commended Ruth's dedication to Naomi and insisted that Ruth glean only in his field so that his workers could protect her (Ruth 2).

4. At Naomi's direction, Ruth presented herself to Boaz in a nighttime encounter in the field and requested that he fulfill the role of family redeemer through the practice of levirate marriage to Ruth. Boaz agreed to do so if a closer relative would not fulfill the role. Boaz later married Ruth, and they had a son whom they named Obed. Obed grew up to become the grandfather of King David (Ruth 3–4).

5. Ruth is the only non-Israelite woman for whom a book of the Bible is named. In Judaism, the story of Ruth is read aloud annually in connection with the Festival of Weeks (Pentecost).

6. Ruth is one of five women (including Mary, Jesus' mother) mentioned in the genealogy of Jesus Christ in Matthew's Gospel (Matt. 1:2-16).

1100–1050 BC	1050–1000
Samuel 1105–1025	Saul chosen as first king of Israel 1050
Saul 1080–1010	David 1040–970
Death of Eli, priest at Shiloh 1070	David becomes king of Judah 1010
Twenty-first Dynasty in Egypt 1069–945	David becomes king of all Israel 1003
Samson defeats enemies in death at Gaza 1060	

The Kinsman Redeemer: His Rights and Responsibilities

By Robert A. Street

The Hebrew noun *go'el* is often translated "kinsman." The word describes a person who has a family responsibility. The Old Testament uses *go'el* in relation to three specific areas of responsibility: property, descendants, and justice. The fourth use of *go'el* is with reference to God as the Redeemer.

Property—Hebrews were not to permanently sell their family or tribal land (see Lev. 25:23). If a brother (family member) sold property, the kinsman was to redeem it (see v. 25). If the brother was too poor to care for himself, the kinsman was to "support him" (v. 35). If the brother sold himself into slavery to a foreigner, he was to be redeemed by his brother, another relative, or by himself by paying the redemption price (see vv. 47-55). Scripture also deals with the redemption of oaths, gifts, and sacrifices (Lev. 27).

Descendants—Ruth provides the example of a kinsman-redeemer ("family redeemer," CSB) in relation to property. The book additionally describes something akin to levirate marriage (see Deut. 25:5-10). Boaz was the kinsman of Naomi through her husband Elimelech (see Ruth 2:1), and of Ruth through her marriage to one of Elimelech's sons. Boaz did not become the kinsman redeemer until the end of the story, when he accepted responsibility for redeeming both the land and Ruth. This marriage was in accord with levirate marriage where a kinsman would marry a relative's widow to ensure the continuance of the relative's name (blood line) in Israel.

Justice—In Numbers 35:19, the *go'el* is "the avenger of blood" (*go'el ha-dam*). When a relative was killed, the kinsman saw to it that justice was carried out. The one accused of the slaying was to flee to one of the cities of refuge. The level of guilt was to be determined there, where the "one who kills someone" was to remain safe as he awaited the congregation to render judgment (see Num. 35:9-12; see also Deut. 19; Josh. 20).

Overlooking the fields of Boaz outside of Bethlehem.

Illustrator Photo/ Jerry Vardaman Collection (29/5/4)

God as Redeemer—The Old Testament depicts the Lord as Redeemer and Vindicator. Many Old Testament passages depict God as the Redeemer (*go'el*) of His people. His removing Israel's oppressions is evident from the exodus through the people's return from Babylonian exile. Using His mighty hand, the Lord redeemed His people from harsh military domination.

The New Testament presents God incarnate, our Kinsman and our Redeemer, Jesus the Christ. As God's children, we are joint heirs with His Son, Jesus Christ (see Rom. 8:17). Further, we have been "redeemed . . . not with perishable things like silver or gold, but with the precious blood of Christ, like that of an unblemished and spotless lamb" (1 Pet. 1:18-19).

Leather sandals; Egyptian; Ptolemaic period 305–30 BC; the kinsman-redeemer sealed his deal with Boaz by taking off his shoe and giving it to Boaz.

Illustrator Photo/ GB Howell/ Cincinnati Museum (35/32/3)

Robert A. Street, "The Kinsman Redeemer: His Rights and Responsibilities," *Biblical Illustrator*, Spring 2016.

Read Ruth 1:11-18.

The story of Ruth is set "during the time of the judges" (Ruth 1:1). The faith displayed in the Book of Ruth contrasts sharply with the accounts of faithlessness in the Book of Judges. Though the Moabites were perennial enemies of Judah, Elimelech was forced to move his family there in search of food during a famine.

After a short time, Elimelech died (see v. 3). His two sons married Moabite women (Ruth and Orpah). Ten years later, the sons died as well (see vv. 4-5). Naomi was left in a foreign land without the support of a husband or sons. The Old Testament world offered little to no support for widows. (By contrast, the Old Testament records numerous passages of God's concern and care for widows; see Deut. 14:28-29; 27:19; Pss. 68:5; 146:9.)

The levirate marriage law meant that Ruth and Orpah could marry only close relatives of Naomi who could stand in the place of her deceased sons. Ruth and Orpah's prospects for finding new husbands were far better if they returned to their family. Then they could marry anyone acceptable to their families and to themselves. The harsh truth for Ruth and Orpah was that their futures were bleak if they remained with Naomi. Naomi released them from this obligation.

Should a believer be ashamed for feeling desperate or distraught? Explain.

It is easy for us to consider Ruth the "good" daughter-in-law and Orpah the "bad" one. In reality, Orpah didn't do anything wrong. She too loved Naomi, wept over her, and kissed her when they parted company. Rather than seeing Orpah as bad, we should see Ruth as extraordinarily loyal and loving.

Ruth "clung" to Naomi (v. 14). The Hebrew word translated "clung" can be interpreted as "bonded." Ruth had bonded with Naomi to the point that she refused to leave. The same word can be used to describe the intimacy of the marriage relationship in that "a man leaves his father and mother and bonds with his wife" (Gen. 2:24).

How does a shared faith create a bond between people? How important is a shared faith among friends?

For the fourth time (see vv. 8,11,12), Naomi pleaded with Ruth to stay in Moab. Ruth gave reasons why it was pointless for Naomi to keep trying to persuade her to leave. Ruth made a lifelong promise to Naomi, insisting she would follow Naomi and live wherever Naomi lived. Remember that Ruth was a Moabite, unlike Naomi the Hebrew. Nevertheless, Ruth vowed that Naomi's people would become her people. Not only did Ruth commit herself to Naomi in life, she committed herself to Naomi in death. The relationship between the two of them could come to an end by one means only—death.

Ruth also declared her allegiance to Naomi's God. In verse 17, Ruth used the personal name of God—Yahweh. Ruth would worship the one true God, the One who created and sustains the universe and set the Israelites free from the bonds of Egyptian slavery.

Ruth was willing to set aside her Moabite identity to join herself to Naomi and her God. Following Naomi and the Lord would involve a renunciation of her past life. In declaring her commitment to Naomi and to the Lord God, Ruth was willing to give up everything.

Ruth exemplified a living and vibrant faith, developed through trials. Ruth's declaration of allegiance to Naomi's God reminds us that faith involves more than just a point of decision; it is a changed way of living that *begins* with a point of decision.

What does a person's response to life's difficulties reveal about what he or she values? How do the difficulties of life sharpen our faith in God?

Read Ruth 2:1-12.

Ruth and Naomi arrived in Bethlehem at the beginning of barley harvest time. Knowing that they needed food to live, Ruth respectfully asked Naomi's permission to go out to the field to gather grain. The Law of Moses required harvesters to leave behind grain that fell in the field so that people in need—foreigners, orphans, or widows—could gather it. Ruth was both a foreigner and a widow, so she was entitled to gather the left-behind grain. Perhaps she wondered how the people would receive her since the Moabites were enemies of the Israelites. But if she and Naomi were to eat, she had to find food somewhere.

When Ruth went out to gather grain, "she happened to be" (v. 3) in a field belonging to Boaz, a relative of her father-in-law Elimelech. The people who lived in the culture of that day would have known that Boaz was a relative of Elimelech. Boaz was known to be a man of wealth and good standing in the community.

What are the implications for believing that events in our lives happen entirely by chance? What are some reasons it might be difficult to believe that nothing happens by chance?

As the story continues, we see Ruth working outdoors to harvest the grain. Because she was willing to do this, she met both Naomi's physical need for food as well as her emotional need of knowing she was cared for and safe. In Ruth, we see a picture of someone who was willing to serve, and serve gladly, with no expectations in return. It's at this time of harvesting grain that we meet Boaz.

Boaz arrived at his field and inquired about the young woman gathering grain. His servants informed him of Ruth's identity. An honorable man, Boaz encouraged Ruth to stay near his female servants and share their water when she was thirsty. Boaz also instructed his male servants not to bother Ruth while she worked. Ruth questioned his kindness toward her, especially since she was a "foreigner" (v. 10).

Ruth may have been a stranger in Bethlehem, but news of her love for Naomi had spread. She had already earned a reputation among the people there. Boaz prayed that God would "reward" Ruth (v. 12). This prayer was a petition for peace and wholeness. Ruth could already see the beginnings of God's rewards at work in her life.

What are some of the attributes of God that Ruth might have leaned on to help her during this time? How does that encourage you?

One of the most important truths about God is that He will take care of us. He will give us the daily bread we need, both physically and spiritually. When we believe God will take care of us, it helps us do things like selflessly serve others in confidence, because we believe we don't actually have to be our own advocate. We have someone wiser and more powerful looking after our interests. In the case of Ruth, God's plan for provision was beginning to unfold through Boaz.

Later in chapter 2, Naomi asked God to bless Boaz because of his kindness (see v. 20). She also explained to Ruth that Boaz was "a close relative. He is one of our family redeemers." According to cultural tradition, when a husband died, his brother (or another family member) assumed responsibility for the deceased man's wife and family. Deuteronomy 25:5-10 states the husband's brother was to marry the widow and name their first male child after the deceased. Perhaps Ruth, a Moabite, did not realize the importance of Boaz as a family redeemer. That would soon become clear.

Read Ruth 3:10–13 and 4:9-17.

Ruth continued to gather grain in Boaz's field throughout the wheat and barley harvests. During these weeks, Naomi observed Boaz's kindness toward Ruth, and she developed a plan for Ruth to show that her mourning had ended and she was ready to return to a social life, perhaps even marriage. Based on cultural traditions of that day, Naomi advised Ruth to present herself in the appropriate way at the appropriate time, and that's what she did.

Boaz knew of Ruth's noble character. In fact, the whole town knew how she had cared for and protected Naomi. Now Boaz, also a person of integrity, was ready to accept the responsibility of family redeemer on Ruth's behalf. He assured Ruth that he would follow the proper steps to secure her future. Accepting responsibility for the physical and spiritual care of family members continues to be God's plan.

In what ways has the world today turned its back on these responsibilities? What can believers do to change the course of these trends?

There was still a problem in the way. Even though Boaz wanted to marry Ruth, there was a closer relative who had the right to do so before Boaz. Boaz promised Ruth he would solve the problem of what to do about the closer relative. He followed the rules out of respect for the legal and cultural requirements of his day.

The city gate was where the citizens carried out administrative and judicial business. Boaz invited this closer relative to discuss the situation there. He also invited the town elders to act as judges and witnesses.

Boaz explained the situation regarding Naomi and her deceased husband Elimelech. This relative, as a family redeemer, had the first right to buy Elimelech's land. If he did not want the land, then Boaz, the next relative in line, intended to purchase it.

The man wanted to buy the land, but he did not want the added responsibility of Naomi and Ruth. He quickly backed out, because it would endanger his own estate. Boaz acted with integrity and resolved the issue legally, so that he could proceed with his offer to redeem Ruth.

How do you see the integrity of Boaz at work here? What are some of the lessons we learn about integrity from his example?

The right of oversight and redemption for the property belonging to Elimelech and his sons passed from the closer relative to Boaz. Boaz and Ruth married, and God blessed them with a son.

In the Book of Ruth, the first description of Naomi portrayed her as a bitter woman who had lost her husband and sons and found herself living in a foreign land. Through God working in her life, the end of the story was totally different. Ruth brought hope to Naomi.

How can the actions of one person bring hope to others? How can carrying out your responsibilities bring hope to another person? Think about specific examples in your life.

The author of Ruth saved the best news for last. Obed, the son of Boaz and Ruth, would grow up to be the grandfather of David, in the family line of Jesus. God didn't just unravel the details in a sad family situation. God unfolded a much greater plan for a Savior right in the middle of the dark days of the judges.

ESTHER
The Brave Deliverer

INTRODUCTION

The Bible is full of men and women who made a difference for God and God's people through acts of courage, sacrifice, or kindness. Some of these people appeared only for a moment in biblical history. They performed their brave acts in the power of the Living God, then withdrew into everyday life. It was as though they were born for just that moment and purpose.

Esther could be described as such a person. Her life was filled with paradoxes: born into the covenant people of God, but grew up in exile outside the promised land; orphaned as a young girl, but raised well by a brave and godly cousin; lived in anonymity one moment, then reigned as the queen of Persia; and enjoyed the luxury of palace life one day, but faced the threat of genocide the next.

While the story of Esther could be read as the story of someone who was either the victim of or the benefactor of circumstances, her story is more than that. It's a testimony of God's specific plan and purpose in the life of an individual. Esther lived and was moved into the right place at the right time by a God who is always in control.

Do you believe that God has a unique plan and purpose for your life? Explain.

Can the majority of your life be explained by any one moment in time? Explain.

Watch the video teaching for Session 6 to discover "The World of Esther," then continue the group discussion.

FOCUS ATTENTION

What was the most interesting fact you learned from the video about the life and times in which Esther lived?

EXPLORE THE TEXT

As a group, read Esther 4:6-9.

Who would you consider an example of how to live a courageous faith in a dangerous place? How can we pray consistently for Christians in dangerous circumstances today?

As a group, read Esther 4:10-12.

Esther's response to Mordecai implied, "Do you realize what you're asking me to do?!" Have you ever wanted to ask God the same question? Explain.

What Scripture passages and biblical examples are comforting for you in times of fear?

How can the courage or fear we display affect the body of Christ as a whole?

As a group, read Esther 4:13-17.

When have you sensed that God positioned you (or another believer) at just the right place and time to do something for His glory?

In what ways was Mordecai's direct statement to Esther in verses 13-14 a turning point for her?

How did God use those days of prayer in Esther's life? How are our lives different when we pray with Esther's kind of urgency?

APPLY THE TEXT

God acted providentially to deliver His people in keeping with His redemptive plan. Believers have the responsibility to act upon the truth we have. Obedience can involve risks, but not as great a risk as failing to obey. We can plead with others to try to help them understand reality. We can take action within God's providence, leaving the results to Him.

What are some of the risks when you hesitate to act on something God is directing you to do?

Who can you depend on to tell you the truth when you need it most? What are you doing to foster that relationship?

In what situations have you tried to control the outcome, instead of trusting the results to God? What steps will you take to relinquish control and trust God completely?

Close your group time in prayer, reflecting on what you have discussed.

ESTHER

KEY VERSE

If you keep silent at this time, relief and deliverance will come to the Jewish people from another place, but you and your father's family will be destroyed. Who knows, perhaps you have come to your royal position for such a time as this.

— Esther 4:14

BASIC FACTS

1. An orphaned Jewish girl among the Babylonian exiles who became the queen of Persia and saved the Jews from a plot of extermination.

2. Jewish name was *Hadassah* [huh DASS uh], meaning "myrtle," or possibly "bride."

3. Name *Esther* is Persian, meaning "star." Unclear if her relative Mordecai [MAWR duh kigh] gave her the name Esther to hide that she was a Jew, or if she received the name when she became a Persian queen.

4. Esther evidently did not give birth to an heir to the Persian throne. The length of her reign as queen is uncertain, although some Bible scholars propose a reign of 13-14 years.

TIMELINE

600–550 BC

- Nebuchadnezzar's invasions of Judah 605, 597, 586
- Ezekiel's prophetic ministry 593–570
- Jerusalem destroyed; Babylonian exile for Jews 586
- Jeremiah forced into exile in Egypt 582

550–500 BC

- Nabonidus rules in Babylon 556–539
- Cyrus rules in Medo-Persia 550–530
- Edict of Cyrus allows Jews to return 538
- Haggai and Zechariah prophecy 520
- Second temple dedicated 516
- Roman republic established 509

KNOWN FOR

1. Esther, a beautiful young Jewish exile in the Persian city of Susa, was an orphan who was adopted and raised by her relative Mordecai. She was selected to become part of the Persian king's harem and quickly became his favorite. The king eventually made Esther his queen (Esth. 2:1-18).

2. Haman, one of the king's top officials, grew violently jealous of Mordecai's favor with the king and plotted to have the king unwittingly sign a decree that called for the extermination of all Jews. Mordecai pleaded with Esther to intervene with the king—even at the risk of her life—to nullify the decree. Esther did as Mordecai asked and saved her people (and herself) by cleverly arranging a meal in which the king learned of Haman's wicked plan (Esth. 3–7).

3. Esther was a woman of great courage and deep spirituality (Esth. 4:16).

4. In Judaism, the Book of Esther is read aloud annually in connection with the Festival of Purim, a celebration of the Jews' rescue from Haman's genocidal plot (Esth. 9:26-32).

500–450 BC

- Xerxes I (Ahasuerus) rules in Persia 486–465
- Esther becomes queen in Persia 479
- Golden age of Greek art 477–431
- Esther saves the Jews from genocide 474
- Malachi's prophetic ministry 460 (early date)
- Ezra leads Jewish exiles to Jerusalem 458

450–400 BC

- Jerusalem's wall rebuilt under Nehemiah 445
- Nehemiah serves as Judah's governor 445–432
- Spartans defeat Athenians 431–404
- Malachi's prophetic ministry 430 (late date)
- Darius II rules in Persia 423-404

The Role of Queen Esther

By Janice Meier

The queen's role can be understood only in conjunction with that of the king. Ahasuerus (also known as King Xerxes, ruled Persia 486-464 BC) typically viewed himself as possessing unlimited personal power, as being above the law, and as displaying great splendor. Xerxes displayed that power in dethroning Queen Vashti, who had failed to appear before him when summoned.

Xerxes's process of selecting a new queen also sheds light on the queen's role (see Esth. 2:1-4,12-14). This procedure reveals that to a large degree, women were merely objects to satisfy a king's personal desires. Obviously, polygamy characterized marital practices in the palace. The Persian king surrounded himself with a large harem of women—some of whom were wives and others, concubines.

Although the women of the harem were isolated and dependent on male favor, a woman nevertheless could wield great power within the palace, particularly if she were selected as queen. Xerxes himself was eventually killed in a harem coup.

Having won King Xerxes's favor, Esther succeeded Vashti as queen (see 2:17). She had faithfully followed her cousin Mordecai's advice not to reveal her identity as a Jew. As the plot of the story unfolds, Haman (Xerxes's prime minister) succeeded in getting the king to issue a decree to destroy the Jews (see 3:8-11). Mordecai urged Esther to approach the king and plead with him for her people's lives (see 4:8). Aware that approaching the king uninvited was a violation of the law and punishable by death, Esther nonetheless courageously entered Xerxes's presence (see v. 16).

Esther invited the king and Haman to a banquet she was hosting. Once there, she revealed Haman's evil plan to kill all of the Jews, which would have included herself, the queen. In explaining Haman's plot, she wisely avoided criticizing the king—who had authorized the genocide. Upon hearing the details, Xerxes was incensed and ordered Haman's immediate execution.

Esther acted prudently within the limitations of her role, yet she also brought a distinct dimension to that role. Because of her faith in God, she dared to step outside the confines of the expected behavioral patterns of a Persian queen when the lives of

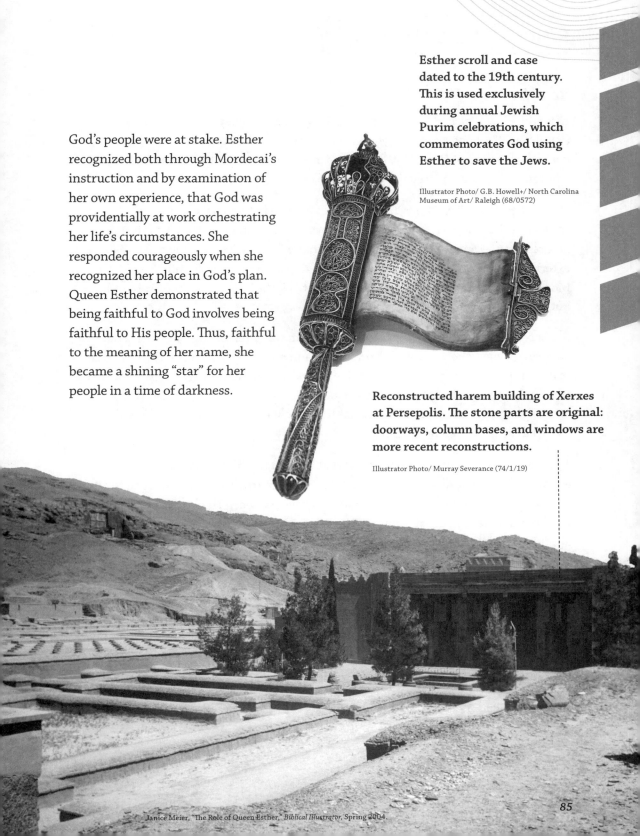

God's people were at stake. Esther recognized both through Mordecai's instruction and by examination of her own experience, that God was providentially at work orchestrating her life's circumstances. She responded courageously when she recognized her place in God's plan. Queen Esther demonstrated that being faithful to God involves being faithful to His people. Thus, faithful to the meaning of her name, she became a shining "star" for her people in a time of darkness.

Esther scroll and case dated to the 19th century. This is used exclusively during annual Jewish Purim celebrations, which commemorates God using Esther to save the Jews.

Illustrator Photo/ G.B. Howell+/ North Carolina Museum of Art/ Raleigh (68/0572)

Reconstructed harem building of Xerxes at Persepolis. The stone parts are original: doorways, column bases, and windows are more recent reconstructions.

Illustrator Photo/ Murray Severance (74/1/19)

Janice Meier, "The Role of Queen Esther," *Biblical Illustrator*, Spring 2004.

Read Esther 3:1-9.

After the king banished his former queen for refusing to obey his summons, Esther found herself among a group of young women being considered as a potential new queen (see 1:10–2:9). When Esther's turn came to meet with Ahasuerus, the king was smitten with her and placed the royal crown on her head (see 2:16-17).

On Mordecai's advice, Esther didn't reveal to anyone in the royal court—including the king—that she was a Jew (see 2:20). However, tension mounted when the king's new second-in-command, Haman, grew furious with Mordecai and devised a plan to exterminate not only him, but also all Jews living in the Persian Empire (see 3:1-9). Mordecai knew that if Haman succeeded in getting the king to sign the death order, not even Queen Esther would be spared.

Ahasuerus inherited one of the largest empires in world history, but he turned out to be a weak leader who was easily manipulated and influenced by others. However, the real villain in the Book of Esther was Haman, a descendant of Agag, a pagan king in the time of Samuel and King Saul of Israel. God had decreed that Agag and his tribe were to be destroyed for their wickedness, but King Saul failed to carry out God's will and spared Agag (see 1 Samuel 15:1-3,8).

The Jews of Esther's day no doubt knew that Haman was a descendant of a sworn enemy of God. King Ahasuerus elevated this evil man to a position of great authority. He became the king's second-in-command. Conflict between Haman and God's people was bound to happen at some point. The only questions were when and what would ignite Haman's fury.

How does a person's past impact his or her present identity?

Previous Persian rulers such as Cyrus showed respect for the religious beliefs of captive peoples (see Ezra 1:2-4). However, King Ahasuerus proved to be less tolerant, having destroyed many groups' temples and shrines in his effort to suppress rebellions.

Haman had little, if any, tolerance, especially for the Jews. Mordecai's refusal to bow down (plus his open confession of being a Jew) would spark a flame that threatened to engulf all of God's people. By extension, God's future plan of salvation in Jesus Christ also would come under attack.

It isn't clear whether Haman noticed Mordecai's defiance prior to being informed. In any case, he took note the next time, and what he saw filled him with rage. The Hebrew term rendered "filled with rage" (v. 5) comes from a root word that means "to be hot, to burn with anger." It pictures an angry heart fueled by selfish pride and an evil determination to get revenge for a perceived slight (see Esther 1:12). Haman's pride fed his rage, which led him to plan unspeakable evil against not only Mordecai but also against God's people, the Jews.

What things make people enraged against God or His people? In what ways can you stand your ground when challenged?

Within these verses lies the principal theme of the Book of Esther: the attempt to destroy God's covenant people, and with their destruction to eliminate the hope of the future Messiah. Haman's plot endangered not only the Jews living in and around Susa, but also those who had returned to Judah—indeed those who lived anywhere in Ahasuerus's kingdom. Haman set in motion an evil plan of empire-wide genocide.

Read Esther 4:6-12.

Hathach was assigned by the king to serve Queen Esther (see 4:5). Esther trusted Hathach, and she sent him to discover what Mordecai was doing—and why. She wouldn't have gone to Mordecai directly at this time, because doing so might have revealed her Jewish identity. Nevertheless, she was concerned about her cousin; he raised her after her parents died (see 2:7). The place where Hathach found Mordecai was an open square outside the entrance gate to the royal palace. This area served as a marketplace; often it was teeming with people.

When have you sought to help someone out of Christlike love only to encounter barriers? How did you overcome the barriers?

Mordecai must have realized by Hathach's questions that Esther knew nothing of the death order. Therefore, he explained all that had happened, including the amount of the bribe Haman paid to secure the king's signature. He also gave Hathach a copy of the decree for Esther. The servant was to explain it to the queen and command her to intercede with the king on behalf of her people. Hathach reported to Esther all that Mordecai told him.

Why is it sometimes difficult to tell others the honest truth about sin's consequences? What is the good news we must also share?

Still using a messenger, both Esther and Mordecai became direct and intense in their speech. Esther's message in 4:11 reveals a new level of authority and maturity. In ancient Persian culture, not even the queen had unrestricted access to the king. She didn't regularly share the king's bed or eat meals with him. Instead, she maintained private quarters with her own attendants.

No one barged into the king's presence without first being summoned by him, not even the queen. Only if the king extended the gold scepter could a person escape the consequences of approaching him uninvited.

Esther had not been summoned to appear before the king for the past thirty days. She realized that the prospect of her being summoned was unlikely. Esther faced a life-and-death dilemma. She needed (and wanted) Mordecai's wise counsel and encouragement before proceeding.

Describe a time when you experienced a dilemma of faith in which the risks of action were high. Who or what helped you decide how to proceed?

What would Esther do? It's a unique situation for sure, but in a sense, it's also a situation that each of us face on a daily basis. At the core, Esther's choice was about self-protection or self-denial. She could walk the road of safety and mind her own business. In so doing, she might have been able not only to conceal her identity, but also to avoid any trouble coming for her people. Or she could choose to be active in the situation. If she chose that route, she would be denying her sense of self-preservation.

Taken like this, Esther's choice is really a mirror of what it means to follow Jesus. Following Jesus means self-denial. It means taking up our cross on a daily basis and going after Him, forsaking our sense of self-protection and self-preservation, and instead relying on God's wisdom, power, and grace for us.

Read Esther 4:13-17.

Mordecai's counsel to Esther contained three elements. First, she needed to realize that her life was under threat whether she approached the king uninvited or did nothing. The death order read that all Jews throughout the empire were to be slaughtered. Mordecai knew that Haman would not rest until every Jew was discovered and slain. This would include Queen Esther.

Second, Mordecai declared a confident belief that deliverance was bound to come for the covenant people. He urged Esther to act boldly and in faith. To falter by denying her Jewish identity at such a time invited divine judgment upon Esther and her deceased father's name and lineage.

Third, Esther was in a strategic position to help God's people. Mordecai again revealed his conviction that God's providential presence and power were in play. God had orchestrated events in Esther's life to position her precisely for this time in history. But she must step forward in faith, trusting in God to advance His kingdom purposes through her.

When have you sensed God positioning you at just the right place and time to do something for His glory?

Esther embraced her God-given purpose. She told Mordecai to lead all the Jews that he could muster from Susa to partake in a three-day fast on her behalf. She and her female attendants also would fast. Fasting in such a desperate situation was a plea for God's miraculous intervention.

Biblical fasting is an act of devotion in which an individual or group puts aside a basic activity of life—eating—in order to focus intently on God and His kingdom. It's a time of seeking spiritual nourishment before physical nourishment. It promotes attitudes of humility, purification, and brokenness before God.

In Scripture, prayer usually accompanied fasting. Even though God's name isn't mentioned directly in this text, there's no doubt God's help was being sought. Esther needed God's involvement. She believed God answered prayer. Like Nehemiah, Esther engaged in prayer and fasting to ask God for success in coming before a non-Israelite king (see Neh. 1:4-11).

Esther already had decided that an act of civil disobedience—yet divine obedience—was the right thing to do, even if it cost her life (compare Daniel 3:16-18). Esther's hesitancy disappeared, replaced by courage. Esther stepped out from her role as Persian queen to become a person of valor, a hero of the faith.

When have you engaged in spiritual disciplines such as prayer and fasting for courage to do something God wanted you to do? What was the result?

Mordecai was satisfied with Esther's decision and instructions. He proceeded to carry out her request.

Chapters 5 through 10 of the Book of Esther tell "the rest of the story." Esther's courageous intervention led to the Jews' deliverance. Haman's wicked scheming led to his execution on the gallows he built for Mordecai's hanging (see 7:10). The Jews were allowed to take vengeance on all who sought to destroy them as God's people (see 8:11). The festival of Purim was established as an annual celebration to remember this event (see 9:20-22). And Mordecai replaced Haman as second-in-command in the Persian Empire (see 10:3).

Esther chose the road of self-denial. In so doing, she "found her life," just as Jesus said all would who forsake themselves to follow Him.

TIPS FOR LEADING A SMALL GROUP

Follow these guidelines to prepare for each group session.

PRAYERFULLY PREPARE

Review

Review the weekly material and group questions ahead of time.

Pray

Be intentional about praying for each person in the group. Ask the Holy Spirit to work through you and the group discussion as you point to Jesus each week through God's Word.

MINIMIZE DISTRACTIONS

Create a comfortable environment. If group members are uncomfortable, they'll be distracted and therefore not engaged in the group experience. Plan ahead by considering these details:

Seating

Temperature

Lighting

Food or Drink

Surrounding Noise

General Cleanliness

At best, thoughtfulness and hospitality show guests and group members they're welcome and valued in whatever environment you choose to gather. At worst, people may never notice your effort, but they're also not distracted. Do everything in your ability to help people focus on what's most important: connecting with God, with the Bible, and with one another.

INCLUDE OTHERS

Your goal is to foster a community in which people are welcome just as they are but encouraged to grow spiritually. Always be aware of opportunities to include any people who visit the group and to invite new people to join your group. An inexpensive way to make first-time guests feel welcome or to invite someone to get involved is to give them their own copies of this Bible study book.

ENCOURAGE DISCUSSION

A good small-group experience has the following characteristics.

Everyone Participates

Encourage everyone to ask questions, share responses, or read aloud.

No One Dominates—Not Even the Leader

Be sure that your time speaking as a leader takes up less than half of your time together as a group. Politely guide discussion if anyone dominates.

Nobody Is Rushed Through Questions

Don't feel that a moment of silence is a bad thing. People often need time to think about their responses to questions they've just heard or to gain courage to share what God is stirring in their hearts.

Input Is Affirmed and Followed Up

Make sure you point out something true or helpful in a response. Don't just move on. Build community with follow-up questions, asking how other people have experienced similar things or how a truth has shaped their understanding of God and the Scripture you're studying. People are less likely to speak up if they fear that you don't actually want to hear their answers or that you're looking for only a certain answer.

God and His Word Are Central

Opinions and experiences can be helpful, but God has given us the truth. Trust God's Word to be the authority and God's Spirit to work in people's lives. You can't change anyone, but God can. Continually point people to the Word and to active steps of faith.

HOW TO USE THE LEADER GUIDE

PREPARE TO LEAD

Each session of the Leader Guide is designed to be torn out so you, the leader, can have this front-and-back page with you as you lead your group through the session. Watch the session teaching video and read through the session content with the Leader Guide tear-out in hand and notice how it supplements each section of the study.

FOCUS ATTENTION

These questions are provided to help get the discussion started. They are generally more introductory and topical in nature.

EXPLORE THE TEXT

Questions in this section have some sample answers or discussion prompts provided in the Leader Guide, if needed, to help you jump-start or steer the conversation.

APPLY THE TEXT

This section contains questions that allow group members an opportunity to apply the content they have been discussing together.

BIOGRAPHY AND FURTHER INSIGHT MOMENT

These sections aren't covered in the leader guide and may be used during the group session or by group members as a part of the personal study time during the week. If you choose to use them during your group session, make sure you are familiar with the content and how you intend to use it before your group meets.

Conclude each group session with a prayer.

SESSION 1 | LEADER GUIDE

FOCUS ATTENTION

Think of a time when you were completely out of your comfort zone. What fears did you have during those moments?

- God gives many strengths and talents to His people, but sometimes He calls us to act in areas where we feel the weakest or least confident, just as He did with Moses. God desires that we remain obedient, trusting Him despite our reluctance or fear.

EXPLORE THE TEXT

Ask a volunteer to read Exodus 3:4-16.

Characterize Moses' initial response when he observed the burning bush and realized something supernatural was happening. When have you realized a situation to be something that only God could do?

- Moses' first response of reverence and fear of the Lord made him attentive to further conversation with God. God first established His identity and His holiness to Moses. Everything else God unfolded and called Moses to do flowed from these foundational truths.

God identified Himself as the God of Moses' father, of Abraham, Isaac, and Jacob. What did this communicate to Moses? How should knowing God's name impact our willingness to follow Him?

- Moses had likely been exposed to many impostor gods in his lifetime. He needed to have firm clarity regarding God's identity as the covenant God of Moses' forefathers.

- God showed Moses this was something bigger than just the present situation. God personally brought Moses into His plan to dwell with His people and bring them into a whole new way of life.

What was the biggest mistake Moses made? How might we make the same mistake today?

- Moses focused more on what God asked of him than on God's character, compassion, and promises. God is at work in the past, present, and future to bring about His will. We can trust that when He invites His people to respond to Him, He is already preparing them as well as working in the circumstances.

Ask a volunteer to read Exodus 4:13-16.

What causes people to hesitate to do what God asks them to do? How do these hesitations compare with Moses' excuses?

- Moses relied on his own ability and gifts rather than on God. We must be careful to obey God, even if He calls us to a task in which we feel inadequate. Often the preparation and strengthening God gives come *after* we surrender to Him. Aaron was on the way before Moses ever knew God sent him to help.

Ask a volunteer to read Exodus 7:1-13.

Why was Moses' and Aaron's exact obedience so important? How does simple and complete obedience demonstrate faith?

- Our disobedience, including our partial obedience, confuses the message from God that He asks us to convey to others. It gives us the false impression that we have the right to pick and choose whether or not to obey Him.

Ask a volunteer to read Exodus 14:21-31.

For the Israelites, what was the result of God working through Moses in such a dramatic fashion?

- Often God asks His followers to trust Him before the outcome is visible. God miraculously made a way for the Israelites to escape to the land He had prepared for them.

What larger impact did the Red Sea crossing and the defeat of Egypt have for Israel? For the surrounding peoples? For believers today?

- Israel had deeply feared their Egyptian overlords for 430 years. Seeing them overwhelmed by God's power changed everything. God's stated intention was for the Egyptians to know He was Yahweh. Knowing He is God is the beginning point to knowing Him (see Ex. 14:4,18).

APPLY THE TEXT

What role does God desire you to play in His redeeming of His people? What steps do you need to take to carry out the mission you have identified?

List resources God has given you to use to accomplish His will. How can you use each resource?

Reflect on Exodus 3:14. In what current situations do you need to be reminded that God is always true to His character?

SESSION 2 | LEADER GUIDE

FOCUS ATTENTION

Many are at least mildly familiar with the story of Jericho. Was there anything in the video that surprised you about the world of Joshua?

- It's important to remember that next to Abraham, Moses was the most significant figure in the lives of the people. Stepping into his shoes would have been no small task for anyone. Surely we can relate to the feelings of anxiety Joshua must have had in doing so.

EXPLORE THE TEXT

Ask a volunteer to read Joshua 6:1-7.

List some instructions that are conspicuously absent for a military campaign such as the one planned. What does the absence of such instructions communicate about God?

- There is no mention of soldiers, and no military strategy is laid out. The people would meticulously execute a ceremony, not expertly wage war. God would win this battle on their behalf.

If the ceremonial actions described in these verses didn't actually accomplish anything, why did the Lord have the Israelites perform them?

- God had already given Jericho into Joshua's hands. Thus, the extensive marching, blowing of trumpets, and shouting that the Israelites were to engage in reinforced for the Israelites that God gave the victory.

Do you think it was easy for Joshua and the Israelites to follow these instructions, given what they were facing? Why or why not?

Ask a volunteer to read Joshua 6:12-21.

As the people prepared to take the city on the seventh day, Joshua gave them an explicit instruction regarding Rahab. Why was she singled out? How did her being protected by Joshua demonstrate God's grace?

- Rahab and all in her house were not to be harmed, because she risked her life to aid God's people. She expressed trust in God by her actions, and grace was extended to her as a result. Joshua functioned as an extension of God in this situation.

What did Joshua direct the people to do with the items in the city? What were the consequences for disobedience? What was the significance of this action?

- The items set aside were to be destroyed. God warned them of the fate that would fall on any who took items from the city for themselves. The silver, gold, and vessels of bronze and iron were to be "dedicated to the LORD" and put into "the LORD's treasury" (v. 19).

Ask a volunteer to read Joshua 6:22-27.

Rahab's obedience to God led to salvation for her whole family. How might God use our obedience to have a great impact on others and bring more glory to Himself?

- Joshua and the people were rewarded with a military victory.

- God rewarded Rahab and her family by protecting them and keeping them safe during battle. Not only did Joshua protect them, but also the future King David came through her lineage. Yet, not just David, but Jesus Christ Himself would descend from Rahab (see Matt. 1:5-6,16).

What has the Lord removed from your life that you have sought to rebuild? Is there something now that God is calling you to give up or not return to again? Why are we often tempted to return to areas where we know life is not found?

APPLY THE TEXT

Where do you feel the Lord calling you to do something you are unsure of? How does this passage encourage you toward obedience, even in the face of doubt?

Consider how Rahab's faith impacted her entire family. How might we extend the grace of God to others so that entire generations might be changed?

In what ways are you tempted to return to parts of your life before Christ, looking for life in dead places? What action will you take to submit this area to God and seek life in Him?

SESSION 3 | LEADER GUIDE

Focus Attention

Have you experienced the challenge of getting a group to buy into a vision? What possible reasons for hesitation exist for following a leader's strategy?

- Some hesitation may be caused by doubts in the strategy or leadership, a selfish attitude, or even a lack of self-confidence. However, when those on a team follow a true leader, they in turn can achieve great things.

- In God, we have the perfect leader; and if we are willing to trust Him, He can do great things in and through us. We see this trust played out in Deborah the Judge.

Explore The Text

Ask a volunteer to read Judges 4:4-10.

The text calls Deborah a "prophetess" acting as a judge. How does this characterization differ from that of other judges in the book? Why is this distinction important.

- In the Old Testament, a prophet or prophetess was a spokesperson for deity to the people. This was not the case for other judges in the book, and is one small but important indicator of how unlikely a judge Deborah was, as prophets were not commonly placed in the role of judge. This might also speak to the inadequacy of the priests to fulfill their rightful roles as mediators between God and man.

Compare and contrast Deborah's role and Barak's role in the management of this crisis. Who looks more like a hero? Explain.

- Deborah is portrayed as a confident and strategic leader. Barak is portrayed as hesitant, if not cowardly. Deborah is insistent, while Barak is resistant.

- Where one might expect a male military leader to play the hero, the female prophetess plays the role in this story.

Ask a volunteer to read Judges 4:11-16.

During the battle, who was credited with causing the victory? How did the victory come about?

- The Lord is given full credit for bringing about the victory over Sisera's army, but not militarily. There is no call to attack. There is only Deborah's declaration that the day for God to deliver Sisera into Barak's hands had arrived.

Ask a volunteer to read Judges 4:17-24.

Verse 24 states that after Sisera's death, "the power of the Israelites continued to increase against King Jabin of Canaan until they destroyed him." Why was this the case? Who in the story were the heroes who made this happen?

APPLY THE TEXT

What did Deborah do remarkably well as a heroine? What lessons can we draw from her story?

What might God be calling you to do that is outside your typical level of comfort or expertise? Pray how God might be working in you to be an unlikely hero.

Barak's hesitation affords an opportunity to evaluate our level of willingness to serve. On a scale of 1 to 10—with 1 being not willing and 10 being actively serving now—how willing are you to give yourself to what God is calling you to do? What evidence can you point to in support of your evaluation? What needs to change for you to increase your level of willingness?

SESSION 4 | LEADER GUIDE

FOCUS ATTENTION

What is the most memorable element of Samson's story to you?

- Samson has one of the most memorable stories in the Bible. It's filled with feats of strength, moments of intrigue, and conquering of enemies. Ultimately, though, the story of Samson is a story of a wasted life.

EXPLORE THE TEXT

Ask a volunteer to read Judges 16:4-6.

What clues do we have that trouble may be on the horizon for Samson?

- Delilah was from the Valley of Sorek in northern Philistia, where the enemies of God's people (the Philistines) lived. Thus, Samson had fallen in love with a Philistine instead of a fellow Israelite as God desired (see Deut. 7:3-4).

- We should be aware of those with whom we create close relationships, as the temptation to fall into spiritual compromise is great. Our closest relationships should be with those who are like-minded in faith and practice.

What does Delilah making a deal with the Philistine leaders reveal about Samson's judgment and the people with whom he chose to associate?

- Delilah began a journey to discover Samson's secret (see v. 6).

- True love is mutual, with both parties putting the needs of the other person ahead of their own. Delilah's motives appear to be less than honorable.

Ask a volunteer to read Judges 16:7-21.

How do you interpret Samson's continuing to offer Delilah the secret to his strength? Do you think he thought this to be a game, or was he simply naive?

- Samson continued to offer Delilah suggestions, as if he was playing a game of cat and mouse with her. Treating the temptation to compromise as a game leads to serious trouble.

How did Delilah's efforts sharpen over time? What does that teach us about the nature of the temptation to compromise?

- Delilah accused Samson of not loving her, upping the pressure on him.

- Temptation to compromise comes in many forms, becoming more acute the closer we get to making an actual compromise.

How did sin blind Samson to the potential disaster awaiting him if he compromised? How does sin blind us?

- Samson's heart became so insensitive to the things of God, that he didn't even realize God's presence had left him.

- James explained that undisciplined and unchecked desires give birth to sin, which grows until that sin causes death (see Jas. 1:14-15).

What might cause a person to lose his or her spiritual sensitivity? How can we guard against losing our spiritual sensitivity?

- Repeated disobedience of God's laws leads to spiritual insensitivity. We can't ignore God in our lives and expect to keep a close relationship with Him.

- We sharpen our spiritual sensitivity when we place consistent priority on our relationship with God (spending time in Bible study, prayer, and worship). Also, we must keep a clean slate by confessing our sin to God.

Ask a volunteer to read Judges 16:28-30.

How did Samson's physical blindness lead to spiritual insight?

- When sight and physical strength were stripped away, Samson turned to God. Samson realized his absolute dependence on God and asked for His help. When we are weak, we tend to understand our need for God with more urgency.

How did God use Samson in spite of his flaws?

- Samson's life revealed many wrong choices and disobedience to God. Yet in the end, God was able to work through Samson despite the flaws. In death, Samson destroyed many Philistines who were the enemies of the Israelites. Read Hebrews 11:32-34 and discuss how God can use flawed people for His purposes.

APPLY THE TEXT

What criteria do you use for determining if you should or should not associate with a person, group, or institution?

What actions can we take to fend off temptation to compromise Christian beliefs? Which of these actions do you need to incorporate into your life?

Reflect on the truth that believers possess the permanent indwelling of the Holy Spirit to equip them to ward off spiritual compromise. How does that truth help you as you face temptation? What are you doing to put yourself in a position to more readily listen to the Holy Spirit?

SESSION 5 | LEADER GUIDE

Focus Attention

Describe a situation in your life that seemed hopeless but turned around for good. How did you see God working through that experience?

- Ruth arrived in Bethlehem with her mother-in-law, Naomi, after the death of both women's husbands. She was a foreigner in a strange land, without even the most basic resources of survival. In the story of Ruth, we see God, in His providence, moving to provide a secure and blessed future.

Explore The Text

Ask a volunteer to read Ruth 3:3-9.

What did Naomi instruct Ruth to do? Why was it important for Ruth to follow Naomi's instructions?

- Naomi told Ruth to wash and anoint herself, put on her cloak, and go to the threshing floor (where Boaz would be). Once he laid down, she was to uncover his feet and lie down as well.

- Naomi instructed Ruth in this manner because she wanted to find security for Ruth (Ruth 1:9). By this, Naomi meant she wanted Boaz to take Ruth as his wife.

When Ruth followed Naomi's directions, what was Boaz's reaction? How did Ruth respond to him?

- In verse 8, we find that he was "startled" and asked, "Who are you?" Ruth told him she was there for him to redeem her.

- There was no immorality in this situation; all the characters were people of high integrity (see v. 11).

What connection did "Take me under your wing" have with Boaz's role as a "family redeemer"? How did the actions of Ruth demonstrate her character?

- "Take me under your wing" (literally, spread the edge of your garment) was an invitation to Boaz that she wanted him to marry her.

- In mentioning his role as a redeemer, Ruth gave the theological basis for seeking Boaz in marriage.

- The family redeemer's (kinsman redeemer) responsibilities were varied, but included continuing the family line (see Deut. 25:5). The practice formally applied to brothers, but apparently was extended in the time of the judges to the nearest kinsman in the family tree.

Ask a volunteer to read Ruth 3:10-17.

How did Boaz respond to Ruth's request?

- Boaz responded by asking God to bless her, thanking her for her kindness to him, and agreeing to do all she asked.

- Boaz also mentioned that there was another redeemer closer than himself, and he would resolve the matter in the morning.

Ask a volunteer to read Ruth 4:9-17.

What was the significance of listing Rachel, Leah, and Tamar in the blessing offered by the witnesses?

- Through Rachel and Leah (and their handmaidens) came the twelve tribes of Israel. Tamar was the mother of Perez, the direct ancestor of Boaz.

- Tamar and Ruth are two of the four women pointed to in the lineage of Jesus in Matthew 1. Boaz's mother was Rahab, the prostitute in Jericho who hid the spies. She was also named in the lineage of Jesus.

Ruth married Boaz, and God blessed them with a son, Obed. How did Ruth become a source of blessing for Naomi? How is she a source of blessing to people today?

- Naomi was blessed because her family had been redeemed. When all seemed hopeless, God provided an heir, a grandson, by His good grace.

- Obed was the grandfather of David, Israel's most beloved king. The world is blessed as Jesus Christ was born from the lineage of Obed (see Matt. 1:5-16). Through Christ, the entire world has been, and will continue to be, blessed.

APPLY THE TEXT

Discuss as a group the value of integrity in relation to our witness. What actions can the group take to foster integrity?

What opportunities is God placing in front of you that come out of trials and challenges you have faced? How can God use those trials and challenges for His honor? Ask Him to help you honor Him in your trials and challenges.

What role do you play in revealing God's redemptive plan to others?

SESSION 6 | LEADER GUIDE

FOCUS ATTENTION

What was the most interesting fact you learned from the video about the life and times in which Esther lived?

- Esther lived during a time when God's people were exiled from the promised land because of their continual idolatry. Despite this, God did not abandon His people. The story of Esther is a reminder that God continues to move and work even in the most trying circumstances.

EXPLORE THE TEXT

Ask a volunteer to read Esther 4:6-9.

Who would you consider an example of how to live a courageous faith in a dangerous place? How can we pray consistently for Christians in dangerous circumstances today?

- Esther faced the possibility of losing her life, but she was the only Jew in the kingdom who placed her life at risk by choice.

Ask a volunteer to read Esther 4:10-12.

Esther's response to Mordecai implied, "Do you realize what you're asking me to do?!" Have you ever wanted to ask God the same question? Explain.

- Life is filled with experiences that can cause us to question the expectations others place on us.

- Through prayer, Scripture, and other believers (such as Mordecai was to Esther), we will be encouraged to be strong and courageous. God won't abandon us.

What Scripture passages and biblical examples are comforting for you in times of fear?

- God gave boldness, conviction, and faith stronger than fear to Joshua, David, Esther, Paul, and so many others—and He does for us as well.

- Esther was hidden in plain sight, because neither Haman nor the king knew she was Jewish. Mordecai asked her to move from relative safety right into the crosshairs—to lay her life down for her people. He wanted her to tap into the faith he had nurtured in her throughout her life.

How can the courage or fear we display affect the body of Christ as a whole?

- If we yield to fear in our Christian lives, the people we influence can get the message that God isn't strong enough to be trusted. Our actions in every area affect the health of the body of Christ.

Ask a volunteer to read Esther 4:13-17.

When have you sensed that God positioned you (or another believer) at just the right place and time to do something for His glory?

- As Christians mature, they begin to understand trials and find opportunities to stand up for the right things as a part of God's larger plan. We see an example of this kind of confidence in Mordecai, who fully believed that God would rescue the Jews from extinction even if Esther chose not to intervene.

- Mordecai knew God had promised to restore them. Understanding God's bigger redemptive story, promises, and plan can help us trust Him confidently.

In what ways was Mordecai's direct statement to Esther in verses 13-14 a turning point for her?

- We need people around us who will not hesitate in telling us the truth.

- There's more at stake than our own plans, comfort, or perspective. God asks us to yield to His plans over our own.

How did God use those days of prayer in Esther's life? How are our lives different when we pray with Esther's kind of urgency?

- God used Esther to deliver His people, reminding them who they were and to Whom they belonged.

- God rescues and is completely able to save. Prayer is a tool God provides as a means of preparing us for His work.

APPLY THE TEXT

What are some of the risks when you hesitate to act on something God is directing you to do?

Who can you depend on to tell you the truth when you need it most? What are you doing to foster that relationship?

In what situations have you tried to control the outcome, instead of trusting the results to God? What steps will you take to relinquish control and trust God completely?

But if it doesn't please you to worship the LORD, choose for yourselves today: Which will you worship—the gods your fathers worshiped beyond the Euphrates River or the gods of the Amorites in whose land you are living? As for me and my family, we will worship the LORD.

JOSHUA 24:15

Whether you're a new Christian or you have believed in Jesus for several years, the people of the Bible have so much wisdom to offer. For that reason, we have created additional resources for churches that want to maximize the reach and impact of the *Characters* studies.

Complete Series Leader Pack

Want to take your group through the whole *Explore the Bible: Characters* series? You'll want a *Complete Series Leader Pack*. This *Pack* includes *Leader Kits* from Volume 1 - Volume 7. It allows you to take your group from The Patriarchs all the way to The Early Church Leaders.

$179.99

Video Bundle for Groups

All video sessions are available to purchase as a downloadable bundle.

$60.00

eBooks

A digital version of the *Bible Study Book* is also available for those who prefer studying with a phone or tablet. Some churches also find eBooks easier to distribute to study participants.

Starter Packs

You can save money and time by purchasing starter packs for your group or church. Every *Church Starter Pack* includes a digital *Church Launch Kit* and access to a digital version of the *Leader Kit* videos.

$99.99 | **Single Group Starter Pack**
(10 *Bible Study Books*, 1 *Leader Kit*)

$449.99 | **Small Church Starter Pack**
(50 *Bible Study Books*, 5 *Leader Kit* DVDs, and access to video downloads)

$799.99 | **Medium Church Starter Pack**
(100 *Bible Study Books*, 10 *Leader Kit* DVDs, and access to video downloads)

$3495.99 | **Large Church Starter Pack**
(500 *Bible Study Books*, 50 *Leader Kit* DVDs, and access to video downloads)

LifeWay.com/characters
Order online or call 800.458.2772.

WANT TO KNOW EVEN MORE ABOUT BIBLICAL CHARACTERS?

The *Explore the Bible: Characters* series features information from the pages of *Biblical Illustrator*. And there are more insights on the way. Every quarter, you'll find remarkable content that will greatly enhance your study of the Bible:

- Fascinating photographs, illustrations, maps, and archaeological finds
- Informative articles on biblical lands, people, history, and customs
- Insights about how people lived, learned, and worshiped in biblical times

Order at lifeway.com/biblicalillustrator or call 800.458.2772.

Continue Your **Exploration**

------------- **VOLUME 3** -------------
THE KINGS

Studying the characters of the Bible helps us understand how God works in the world, loves His people, and moves through His people to accomplish His plans. The next volume of *Explore the Bible: Characters* focuses on Saul, David, Solomon, Asa, Hezekiah, and Josiah. Build on your new knowledge of the Old Testament Heroes and study the history of its kings.

Bible Study Book 005823505 **$9.99**
Leader Kit 005823538 **$29.99**

EXPLORE YOUR OPTIONS

EXPLORE THE BIBLE

X **EXPLORE THE BIBLE.**

If you want to understand the Bible in its historical, cultural, and biblical context, few resources offer the thoroughness of the Explore the Bible ongoing quarterly curriculum. Over the course of nine years, you can study the whole truth, book by book, in a way that's practical, sustainable, and age appropriate for your entire church.

6- TO 8-WEEK STUDIES

If you're looking for short-term resources that are more small-group friendly, visit the LifeWay website to see Bible studies from a variety of noteworthy authors, including Ravi Zacharias, J.D. Greear, Matt Chandler, David Platt, Tony Evans, and many more.

Prices and availability subject to change without notice.